the Hungry Heart

the Hungry Heart

Daily Devotions from the Old Testament

JAN CARLBERG

Wolgemuth & Hyatt, Publishers, Inc.
Brentwood, Tennessee

The mission of Wolgemuth & Hyatt, Publishers, Inc. is to publish and distribute books that lead individuals toward:

- A personal faith in the one true God: Father, Son, and Holy Spirit;
- A lifestyle of practical discipleship; and
- A worldview that is consistent with the historic, Christian faith.

Moreover, the Company endeavors to accomplish this mission at a reasonable profit and in a manner which glorifies God and serves His Kingdom.

Published March 1991. First Edition.
Printed in the United States of America.
97 96 95 94 93 92 91   8 7 6 5 4 3 2 1

Wolgemuth & Hyatt, Publishers, Inc.
1749 Mallory Lane, Suite 110
Brentwood, Tennessee 37027

Library of Congress Cataloging-in-Publication Data

Carlberg, Jan, 1940–
The hungry heart : daily devotions from the Old Testament / Jan Carlberg, —1st ed.
p. cm.
ISBN 1-56121-051-X
1. Bible. O.T.—Devotional use. 2. Devotional calendars.
I. Title.
BS1151.5.C365 1991
242′.2—dc20

90-26610
CIP

Dedicated to
my parents,
Harold and Margaret Jensen;
parents-in-love,
Robert and Helen Carlberg.

And

In memory of
my grandparents,
Elias and Ella Tweten;
grandparents-in-love,
Carey and Elizabeth Thomas,
who practiced in the home, then
preached from pulpit, street corner, tent,
radio, and person to person the truths of
the Bible. Their example encouraged a
hunger in me to love God and
to know His Word.

Since my youth, O God, you have taught me, and to this day I declare your marvelous deeds. Even when I am old and gray, do not forsake me, O God, till I declare your power to the next generation, your might to all who are to come.

(Psalm 71:17–18)

CONTENTS

Acknowledgments

To my husband, Judson, for pushing me out of the nest and encouraging me to fly, for teaching me to use the computer, for listening and for loving me when I flew, crawled, or simply sat.

To our children, Heather and Chad, for challenging me to think and look at old truths from the perspective of their generation.

To my parents, who believed in me before I believed in myself.

To my brother Ralph and sister-in-love, Chris, for cheers along this runner's route.

To the women of JOY Bible Study for exposing their hungry hearts and encouraging me to share God's food.

To friends who nudged with notes, counsel, or listening hearts: Harold and Carol Bussell, Marilyn Bullock, Judith Bynum, Dottie Colby, Linda and Neil Cornell, Stan Gaede, Dave Horn, Marty and Dale Lefever, Debbie Lentz, Mary Macaluso, Steve Macchia, Gordon and Gail MacDonald, Joanna Mockler, Bill and Carolyn Wilkie and for my Council for Independent Colleges' friends: Florence Anglin, Gretchen Bearce, Esther Blankenbaker, Melva Brandt, Jean Forbes and MaryAnn Rehnke.

To those in the writing and publishing profession whose experience and encouragement supported me for this adventure: Wayne Hastings, Bill Petersen, Les Stobbe, Doug Weaver and the superb team at Wolgemuth and Hyatt.

JANUARY

JANUARY 1

And God said, "Let there be light," and there was light. Genesis 1:3

Further reading: Genesis 1:1–5

During the long, dark days of winter, what a lift to body and spirit to sit by the light of a fire, to read by a lamp, to eat by candlelight. Peering into the unknowns of a new year, what a faith-lifter to know, "You are my lamp, O LORD; the LORD turns my darkness into light." 2 Samuel 22:29

Question: What darkness do you dread today?

Faithlift: Today, the light of God's presence walks with you, enabling you to challenge and conquer darkness within and without.

JANUARY 2

God had finished the work he had been doing, so on the seventh day he rested from all his work. Genesis 2:2

Further reading: Genesis 1–2:3

Too often our church and culture suffer from Same Day Syndrome. Our days run together in a blur of frenzied activity, deadlines, incomplete to-do lists, and a gnawing sense that there must be a better way. There is! It's called the Sabbath Day. A Sabbath admits we are dispensable and dependent on God for our work and rest. God says, "If you keep your feet from breaking the Sabbath and from doing as you please on my holy day . . . if you honor it by not going your own way and not doing as you please or speaking idle words, then you will find your joy in the LORD." Isaiah 58:13–14

Question: Do you experience true Sabbath rest, or is Sunday one more work day with a variation or two?

Faithlift: A Sabbath per week adds up to almost two months of true rest and reflection, worship and thanksgiving, each year. Talk about worker's benefits!

JANUARY 3

Then God opened her eyes and she saw a well of water. Genesis 21:19

Further reading: Genesis 21:1–21

Hagar the homeless and her son Ishmael present a stark portrait of despair and futility. They wandered in a desert, out of water and worse, out of hope. Who would hear the sobs and notice one little homeless family? "God heard the boy crying, and the angel of God called to Hagar . . . 'Do not be afraid. . . .' Then God opened her eyes and she saw a well of water" (Genesis 21:17–19). This was no mirage; this was a miracle handled by ministering angels of our loving Father God. They drank, and "God was with the boy as he grew up" (v. 20).

Question: What is your desert of despair, your place of parched hopelessness?

Faithlift: The God of Hagar and Ishmael sees and hears you in your desert. He waits to sustain and refresh you today with living water.

JANUARY 4

But while he was still living, he gave gifts. Genesis 25:6

Further reading: Genesis 25:1–11

The bills of Christmas, winter-bleak bearers of accounts of enthusiastic or duty-bound shopping, pile up like yesterday's newspapers. Are we pawns of clever marketing or duty-bound shoppers? Do we give out of love and thankfulness? Abraham gave gifts while he was alive; he was thoughtful to those who were close to him.

Question: Is your lack of generosity or your gift-giving killing more than your budget?

Faithlift: Recall three gifts you have freely received from God today. Thank Him and freely give a duty-free gift to someone else.

JANUARY 5

While Joseph was there in the prison, the LORD was with him. Genesis 39:20–21

Further reading: Genesis 39

Joseph had done nothing to warrant being in Egypt or in prison. His brothers had betrayed him and sold him to some merchants en route to Egypt. A prominent Egyptian bought Joseph, who soon became a trusted servant. But the owner's wife lusted after young Joseph; and when Joseph resisted her advances, she slandered him, and her husband threw him into prison. One day Joseph was the favored son, dressed in a richly ornamented robe. Not long after, he wore prison garb. Where was God during these unjust days of a young Jewish man's life? "The LORD was with him; he showed him kindness and granted him favor in the eyes of the prison warden" (v. 21).

Question: Can you believe God is with you in your prison?

Faithlift: David in Psalm 139 reminds us that there is nowhere we can go where God's presence will not be. That includes your prison.

JANUARY 6

When all goes well with you, remember me and show me kindness. Genesis 40:14

Further reading: Genesis 40

Joseph was in prison. Two long years had passed since his fellow prisoner, the king's cupbearer, had been released.

The cupbearer was to have remembered Joseph, but Joseph's name had not even come up in conversation between the cupbearer and Pharaoh. Then the king had a dream which no one could interpret. The cupbearer recalled the young Hebrew Joseph, who interpreted dreams. The past two good years for the cupbearer had dulled his memory of his imprisoned friend. Regretfully, he informed the Pharaoh, "Today I am reminded of my shortcomings" (Genesis 41:9).

Question: When times turn for the better, do you remember to keep commitments you made while a fellow sufferer?

Faithlift: "The LORD is faithful to all his promises and loving toward all he has made." Psalm 145:13

JANUARY 7

I have heard it said of you . . .
Genesis 41:15

Further reading: Genesis 41:1–40

When your name comes up, what do people say? The mighty but troubled Pharaoh had heard that a prisoner named Joseph could interpret dreams. He sent for Joseph, and a prison guard lumbered down the dank steps to get him. Joseph's eyes, geared to the dungeon's darkness, blinked and burned at the light. He washed, shaved, changed his clothes, and prepared to meet the most powerful man in the world. What an opportunity for Joseph, the powerless, to be needed by Pharaoh, the powerful! Young Joseph must have been tempted to seize this opportunity to make himself indispensible to the king. But the dungeon's darkness had not dimmed his awareness of who gave him the wisdom to interpret dreams and who had plans for his life. And so to Pharaoh Joseph responded, "I cannot do it." Imagine! Young Joseph went on to give proper credit to the God who would "give Pharaoh the answer he desire[d]" (Genesis 41:16).

Question: Are you willing to publicly acknowledge the wisdom and work of God in your life today?

Faithlift: You are not a powerless person. God and you are a strong team today.

JANUARY 8

Don't be afraid. Am I in the place of God? Genesis 50:19

Further reading: Genesis 50:1–21

Guilt and fear choked Joseph's brothers when they saw that their father was dead. Rightful dread formed words and whispers. "What if Joseph holds a grudge against us and pays us back for all the wrongs we did to him?" They sent word to Joseph, "Your father left these instructions before he died: . . . I ask you to forgive your brothers the sins and the wrongs they committed in treating you so badly." Then they added their own confession, "Now please forgive the sins of the servants of the God of your father." Joseph's response? He wept.

He wept? This was his opportunity to repay them for his suffering. They threw themselves at his feet, offered themselves as servants, and Joseph wept! Vulnerable, not victorious, Joseph reassured his broken brothers. "Don't be afraid. Am I in the place of God? You intended to harm me, but God intended it for good to accomplish what is now being done, the saving of many lives. So then, don't be afraid. I will provide for you and your children."

Question: What will you lose if you make yourself vulnerable to a brother or sister? What will you gain if you are victorious?

Faithlift: Look for God's good in the bad times you've experienced.

JANUARY 9

The midwives, however, feared God and did not do what the king of Egypt had told them to do; they let the boys live. Exodus 1:17

Further reading: Exodus 1

There is a place for civil disobedience, a time to rise up and go counter-culture. The time is when people in authority demand that we disobey God's law. We live in an unredeemed, un-Christian culture, but that alone does not warrant civil disobedience. God's Word teaches, "Everyone must submit himself to the governing authorities, for there is no authority except that which God has established. . . . Give everyone what you owe him: If you owe taxes, pay taxes; if revenue, then revenue; if respect, then respect; if honor, then honor" (Romans 13:1, 7). What remarkable women of faith, these unnamed Hebrew midwives who defied the king's command to kill baby boys and instead obeyed God's higher law of love.

Question: Are you willing to go counter-culture and fear God more than those who would disagree with your stance?

Faithlift: No one is too insignificant to make a difference. "He helps me do what honors Him the most" (Psalm 23:3, The Living Bible).

JANUARY 10

And God said, "I will be with you." Exodus 3:12

Further reading: Exodus 3 and 4:17

Moses, murderer-in-exile and shepherd, conversed with the God of heaven and earth. From within a burning bush God spoke to Moses concerning the suffering of His children in Egypt. Moses struggled to believe God's choice of leadership. Even after God's miraculous signs of power—turning his staff into a snake and causing his hand to turn leprous and restoring it to health again—Moses battled to believe. To convince this persistent God, Moses stammered, "O Lord, I have never been eloquent, neither in the past nor since you have spoken to your servant. I am slow of speech and tongue" (Exodus 4:10). Moses, listed in the

Hebrews 11 Hall of Faith, stood fearful and faithless before his all-powerful God. Looking at himself, Moses panicked instead of listening to God promise His presence and power. When we look to ourselves only, we, too, are insufficient to do God's work.

Question: As you look to an impossible challenge today, are God's promises sufficient?

Faithlift: Moses, once fearful and faithless, grew on to be one of God's faithful sons. We, too, will grow in our faith through simple obedience.

JANUARY 11

Moses answered the people, "Do not be afraid." Exodus 14:13

Further reading: Exodus 14

How much time elapsed between the time Moses fearfully looked at himself and declined God's command to lead and the time he stood with his back to the Red Sea and said to the children of Israel, "Do not be afraid"? Enough time for Moses to have experienced God's power through many encounters with Pharaoh. Enough time for Moses to have embraced God's persevering love for His children. Enough time that, with his back against a wall of water, Moses shouted bold encouragement to his people who were so full of the fears he remembered too well. He bellowed, "Stand firm and you will see the deliverance the LORD will bring you today. The Egyptians you see today you will never see again. The LORD will fight for you; you need only to be still." And all he spoke came true.

Question: Will you believe less in your faithlessness and more in God's faithfulness today?

Faithlift: Moses and God's children walked through that Red Sea. They didn't swim one stroke! They didn't need fins, tubes, or rafts! God walks today with you through your rough waters.

JANUARY 12

You are not grumbling against us, but against the LORD. Exodus 16:8

Further reading: Exodus 16

Grumbling, that steady rumble of discontent, revealed the hearts of the Israelites, just as it exposes ours. It didn't take long to get over the miracle of the Red Sea. Three days of desert trekking without water eradicated the miracle and illuminated their misery. Like us, they targeted the leaders. "You have brought us out into this desert to starve this entire assembly to death" (Exodus 16:3). Moses reminded this collection of murmurers that they were really upset with God. "Who are we? You are not grumbling against us, but against the LORD." And how did God respond to His children? With compassion! "I will rain down bread from heaven for you . . . at twilight you will eat meat . . . then you will know that I am the LORD your God" (Exodus 16:4, 12). Those grumblers got what they didn't deserve: grace!

Question: Where is your focus today—on the miracles or on the misery?

Faithlift: As you eat your bread and meat today, do more than say grace; give grace to those around you. "Freely you have received, freely give" (Matthew 10:8).

JANUARY 13

What is this you are doing for the people? Exodus 18:14

Further reading: Exodus 18

Jethro, Moses' father-in-law, observed a day in the life of Moses. From morning until evening people pressed Moses, the judge, with their disputes. He decided and "inform[ed] them of God's decrees and laws." But Jethro, unimpressed with Moses' system, gave a gift that kept on giving: simple truth. "The work is too heavy for you; you cannot handle it alone." Jethro then outlined a plan of administration and delegation that freed Moses for major cases, affirmed and grew other leaders, and satisfied the people. How easily we get tricked into thinking we have to do it all! How refreshing to have a family member or friend to ask the hard questions, speak truth, and offer an alternate plan! And how wise of Moses, who "listened to his father-in-law and did everything he said."

Question: How are you responding to someone's gift of simple truth?

Faithlift: A teachable heart grows wise, not old.

JANUARY 14

You are a stiff-necked people. Exodus 33:5

Further reading: Exodus 33

God spoke truth to the children of Israel. While Moses had been on Mount Sinai receiving the Ten Commandments from God, God's children and Moses' brother Aaron had cast a golden calf—a gilded god. As a consequence, three thousand died, a plague moved through the camp, and God decided to remove His presence from His people. How sinfully stiff-necked to "prefer the presence of an ox that eats grass to the glorious presence of God Himself" (Psalm 106:19–20, The Living Bible).

Question: In what ways are you stiff-necked, preferring something or someone to God?

Faithlift: God desires your company today. You need not go through this day alone.

JANUARY 15

If your Presence does not go with us, do not send us up from here. Exodus 33:15

Further Reading: Exodus 33

Moses journeyed an even greater distance spiritually than physically. During the years of inching on by faith, Moses learned the true indispensables of life. While the children of Israel seemed preoccupied with life's fringe benefits, Moses focused on knowing, obeying, and depending on God. As Moses thought about moving this collection of thankless, rebellious people toward the Promised Land, he knew there was only one thing in life that was truly non-negotiable: the presence of God. "If your Presence does not go with us, do not send us up from here . . . . What else will distinguish me and your people from all the other people on the face of the earth" (Exodus 33:15–16)?

Question: Are you making spiritual as well as physical progress as you move through this day?

Faithlift: God's promise to Moses is for us, too. "My Presence will go with you, and I will give you rest" (Exodus 33:14).

JANUARY 16

The LORD has chosen Bezalel son of Uri . . . and he has filled him with the Spirit of God, with skill, ability and knowledge in all kinds of crafts. Exodus 35:30–31

Further reading: Exodus 35

Three cheers and more for the Bezalel's on this earth—men and women whom God has filled with those skills that add beauty to our world. Sometimes within the church we prize gifts that seem more spiritual, such as teaching and preaching, and neglect to celebrate the creativity God gives to artists, sculptors, metalsmiths, woodcarvers, and needleworkers. Bezalel and his co-worker, Oholiab, combined their skill to do the work with the ability to teach others. As a result, many hands trained and united to build a sanctuary for God.

Question: How do you show your appreciation for God's unique gifts in yourself and in others?

Faithlift: "Each one should use whatever gift he has received to serve others, faithfully administering God's grace in its various forms"

(1 Peter 4:10). Fully, joyfully using God's gift in you for others is your gift to God.

JANUARY 17

You must distinguish between the holy and the profane, between the unclean and the clean. Leviticus 10:10

Further reading: Leviticus 10

Often the lines are fuzzy between the holy and the profane in our culture. And the church sometimes adds to the confusion. Aaron's sons, Nadab and Abihu, paid with their lives for taking God's commands lightly. We would do well to listen carefully and to obey quickly when God speaks. While we may not die immediately when we disobey, signs of sin-sickness gnaw at our spirits and inhibit real life.

Question: Do I confuse others who seek an example of holy living?

Faithlift: The wisdom of God in me sees the distinctions; the life of God in me empowers me to live His standards for holiness.

JANUARY 18

The alien living with you must be treated as one of your native-born. Leviticus 19:34

Further reading: Leviticus 19

There's something deep within us that loves to be first, to win, to be "in." We elbow up through degrees, titles, possessions, rights, privileges, connections, seniority, and the like. But once we reach our goals, then what? God doesn't separate us from those who are lower on the career ladder than we are. He tells us to pull them up with us. "Love him as yourself, for you were aliens in Egypt. I am the LORD your God" (Leviticus 19:34). In a few words God both levels and lifts us: "You were an alien, too," and "I am your Lord God."

Question: Is there an alien who needs my lift today?

Faithlift: God's words may level us but they also lift. Look for the lift.

JANUARY 19

Do not take advantage of each other, but fear your God. I am the LORD your God.
Leviticus 25:17

Further reading: Leviticus 25

How soon we forget! Such a short time ago the children of Israel were slaves in Egypt. They had been taken advantage of by their masters. Now, freed by the Egyptians and en route to the Promised Land, they were still bound by sinful tendencies to want to master others. Years of brickmaking had calloused more than hands. God, our generous Father, spelled out His rules for righteous living. Simply put, the rules said "don't take advantage of each other, but fear your God." What lesser gods do we fear enough to exploit another human being? Perhaps we fear the gods of success, materialism, status, self-protection. When pressed, any one of us is apt to bow to a lesser god. How different our world would be if we obeyed this simple truth: "Do not take advantage of each other."

Question: As you look at your relationships with others, which gods (God) do you fear?

Faithlift: "The fear of the LORD is the beginning of wisdom" (Psalm 111:10).

JANUARY 20

We remember the fish we ate in Egypt at no cost . . . but now we have lost our appetite; we never see anything but this manna!"
Numbers 11:5–6

Further reading: Numbers 11

God had miraculously delivered the Israelites from the hands of cruel masters, yet this phenomenal act paled as the people faced eating another bowl of manna. How like those children of Israel we really are! The high cost of obedience and a thankful heart looks exorbitant beside the offerings of the world. The test of our love for God is in our heart's attitude toward His ordinary provisions, His day-in, day-out manna of grace and love. Ultimately, we'll pay dearly for the world's "fish." We were made for manna.

Question: Have you lost your appetite for manna?

Faithlift: Praise the God who provides you with "manna" today in your "wilderness."

JANUARY 21

Miriam and Aaron began to talk against Moses. Numbers 12:1

Further reading: Numbers 12

Moses, surrounded by complaining Israelites, received cruel, unwarranted criticism from within his own family. His sister and brother huddled, mumbled, and compared themselves to Moses. "Hasn't God also spoken through us?" Such jealousy and self-exaltation may have missed Moses' ears, but God heard. God summoned the three of them to meet Him at the entrance to the Tent of Meeting, and their all-knowing Father made a clear distinction between Moses and his siblings. "With Moses I speak face to face . . . . Why then were you not afraid to speak against my servant Moses?" That is a good question. Why weren't they afraid? And why aren't we afraid to be so critical? God's tough love for this family triangle showed in consequences (Miriam turned leprous), confession (Aaron, abased, pled for God's and Moses' forgiveness and for Miriam's healing), and commitment to restoration (Moses interceded with God for Miriam's healing). In Numbers we read, "and the people did not move on till [Miriam] was brought back" (12:15). Until the loop has been closed on our ruptured relationships, their healing and ours stalls. We will not move on until our Miriam is brought back.

Question: Are you Moses or Miriam today?

Faithlift: The Father who defended Moses and disciplined Miriam is our Father, too. He will help us restore broken relationships and bridle a critical tongue so we and they can move on.

JANUARY 22

We seemed like grasshoppers in our own eyes. Numbers 13:33

Further reading: Numbers 13

Most of the spies Moses sent to explore the Promised Land came back with a warped perspective. While all the spies saw the land flowing with milk and honey, only two saw it as possessed by God. The majority saw the obstacles; the minority saw the opportunities. The fearful saw the land peopled with giants. The faithful saw the land promised by God. The fearful saw themselves as grasshoppers. The faithful saw God as protector. The issue was not the size of the people but the measure of their God.

Question: Are you focused more on giants than on God?

Faithlift: "I am the LORD, the God of all mankind. Is anything too hard for me?" (Jeremiah 32:26)

JANUARY 23

Wouldn't it be better for us to go back to Egypt? Numbers 14:3

Further reading: Numbers 14

Miracles aren't enough for most of us when God's ways and ours collide. The Israelites sat perched on the edge of the Promised Land, but grumbling, not gratitude, poured out of their hearts. Moses, Aaron, Joshua, and Caleb neither manipulated nor murdered their cowardly congregations. They mourned! They tore their clothes, fell face down in front of the people, and mourned. Then they pled with them to shift their focus from their fears to God's faithfulness. They reiterated how exceedingly good the land was and how great their God. "Do not be afraid of the people of the land, because we will swallow them up. Their protection is gone, but the LORD is with us. Do not be afraid of them" (Numbers 14:9). Fear of the unknown muddied the past and once again made Egypt look like the Promised Land to many of the Israelites. The familiar, no matter how bad, seemed safer.

Question: What is your Egypt—your place of faithless familiarity?

Faithlift: Your unknowns are known to God. He walks with you today as you resist the temptation to retreat to Egypt.

JANUARY 24

The LORD replied, "I have forgiven them, as you asked."
Numbers 14:20

Further reading: Numbers 14

How do you respond when your enemies repeatedly assassinate your character, challenge your authority, and negate your leadership? Moses enjoyed few respites from complaining children after he became their reluctant leader. But their slander did not dull his awareness of their real target: God Himself! It was God who heard the cries of His people in Egypt. It was God who recruited Moses! It was God who led them away from familiar bondage to freedom's borders! It was God who set up a menu of manna! It was God whom they resented at the core! So Moses did not pray, "Oh God, turn their hearts toward me. Help them to respect me as their leader. You got me into this; get me out or leave me in with a bonus or two." Moses' thoughts were not focused on himself; instead, they turned toward God and God's children. To God's righteous anger against His children, Moses pleaded, "The Egyptians will hear about it! . . . The nations . . . will say, 'The LORD was not able to bring these people into the land he promised them on oath. . . .' In accordance with your great love, forgive the sin of these people, just as you have pardoned them for the time they left Egypt until now" (Numbers 14:13, 15–16, 19). And God listened to Moses and forgave the repeat offenders.

Question: How will you respond to the repeat offenders in your life today?

Faithlift: Forgiveness honors God and heals you.

JANUARY 25

But they said, "We will not come!" Numbers 16:12

Further reading: Numbers 16

Rebellion of the heart eventually shows in outward acts. Dathan, Korah, and Abiram assembled about 250 well-known Israelite leaders who then slithered toward Moses and blasted the leadership of brothers Aaron and Moses. When Moses singled out Dathan and Abiram for a face-to-face talk, they retorted, "We will not come! Isn't it enough that you have brought us up out of a land flowing with milk and honey to kill us in the desert? And now you also want to lord it over us?" (vv. 12–13)

Rebellion distorts reality. Egypt now looked like the Promised Land "flowing with milk and honey," and Moses seemed a punitive taskmaster. The next day the earth opened and swallowed these rebellious men and their families. Rebellion is always costly to more than just the rebel.

Question: Have you ever dug in your heels and said, "I will not come!"?

Faithlift: God came to us through His Son, Jesus Christ. His coming makes it possible for us to come to God or others to make things right.

JANUARY 26

Then the LORD opened the donkey's mouth, and she spoke to

Balaam, "What have I done to you?" Numbers 22:28

Further reading: Numbers 22

What a hilarious scene, a wise donkey and a foolish master conversing! Stunned Balaam, hand stinging from beating his donkey, jabbered with his jackass. How foolish the donkey had made him appear by refusing to clop on down that road! The long-lashed donkey lifted sad eyes and asked, "Am I not your own donkey, which you have always ridden, to this day? Have I been in the habit of doing this to you?" (v. 30) A slow, whiny "no" must have slipped from red-faced Balaam's tongue. Then God opened Balaam's eyes to see the angel of the Lord—a winged roadblock obvious only to his beast of burden. Balaam swiftly confessed his sin and commited to God's way. And the donkey enjoyed the last hee haw.

Question: Are you beating someone else for your own disobedience?

Faithlift: Obey today and miss a donkey's bray.

JANUARY 27

. . . so the LORD's people will not be like sheep without a shepherd. Numbers 27:17

Further reading: Numbers 27:12–23

Moses, great leader and God's good friend, moved slowly up the mountain to let his eyes experience what his feet would never touch: the Promised Land. Because he disobeyed God's specific command at the waters of Meribah, Moses received swift and stern consequences. "Because you did not trust in me enough to honor me as holy in the sight of the Israelites, you will not bring this community into the land I give them" (Numbers 20:12). But we see the measure of this man in the way he handled God's discipline, without a whimper or a complaint. He never caught grumbler's fever from the children he led to the border of the Promised Land. As he faced death, Moses focused on the people he had led, not on the Promised Land he would never touch. He interceded once again for God's people. "May the LORD, the God of the spirits of all mankind, appoint a man over this community to go out and come in before them, one who will lead them out and bring them in, so the LORD's people will not be like sheep without a shepherd." Moses, a true servant-leader, was never greater than when he was bowing in prayer on behalf of God's children. He exited by interceding and installing the next shepherd who would lead the sheep he loved so well.

Question: Do you love the sheep in your field enough to intercede?

Faithlift: The Good Shepherd intercedes with love for you.

JANUARY 28

But commission Joshua, and encourage and strengthen him. Deuteronomy 3:28

Further reading: Deuteronomy 3:21–29

Moses had faced one challenge after another with God's grumbling sheep. Now he was pressed to put his heart into his own farewell. Moses didn't simply pack up his staff and rip his sign off his tent flap, nor pray for his successor, then exit. God told Moses to lay hands on Joshua, but his responsibilities didn't even end with the commissioning service. God then pressed His friend Moses to move from the service of commissioning to the sacrifice of encouraging and strengthening Joshua. God called Moses to put heart into his farewell. Love launched Joshua!

Question: Who needs your sacrifice of encouragement today?

Faithlift: God makes His heart visible to, then through, you.

JANUARY 29

These commandments that I give you today are to be upon your hearts. Impress them on your children. Deuteronomy 6:6–7

Further reading: Deuteronomy 6

Someone wisely said that truths are better caught than taught. Examples speak clearly. Moses moved the people to understand that the basis for doing and teaching was their love for God. When they loved the Lord with all their "heart, soul and strength," they would want to store His words in their hearts and impress His words on their children. It would be natural to talk about God's laws "when [they sat] at home and when [they walked] along the road, and when [they laid] down and when [they got] up." Perhaps we fumble around with family devotions because we teach God's truths before we've caught them ourselves.

Question: Have God's words marked you before you attempt to impress them on others?

Faithlift: God gives us wisdom and strength to know His words, to follow Him, and to lead by example.

JANUARY 30

When you have eaten and are satisfied, praise the LORD *your God. Deuteronomy 8:10*

Further reading: Deuteronomy 8

Prosperity challenges us to praise God. We're not so unlike the children of Israel that we can shuffle these words aside as belonging to another culture. It is a continual challenge to maintain a thankful heart. When all our needs and wants are met, to whom do we give the credit? Moses reminded those who, like us, were sure they would never forget God's goodness, "When you have eaten and are satisfied, praise the LORD your God for the good land he has given you. Be careful that you do not forget the LORD your God, failing to observe his commands, his laws and his decrees that I am giving you this day. Otherwise, when you eat and are satisfied, when you build fine houses and settle down, and when your herds and flocks grow large and your silver and gold increase and all you have is multiplied, then your heart will become proud and you will forget the LORD your God, who brought you out of Egypt, out of the land of slavery" (Deuteronomy 8:10–14). Prosperity challenges us to focus on God, not goods.

Question: Is your focus on the Provider or on the provisions?

Faithlift: Praise and thank God for providing your needs today.

JANUARY 31

I did this so that you might know that I am the LORD your God.
Deuteronomy 29:6

Further reading: Deuteronomy 29

Forty years had passed from the time the Israelites left Egypt until they camped on Canaan's sand. Disobedience delayed them as a people from a direct trek to the Promised Land. Death, natural or supernatural, removed some individuals from the Promised Land. Now their children and grandchildren listened to Moses reiterate God's faithfulness—from where they had walked to what they had worn. The magnitude of the Red Sea crossing made the mundane matter of everlasting clothes and sandals seem insignificant. Yet their great Provider reminded them that He would miss no detail concerning their needs. "During the forty years that I led you through the desert, your clothes did not wear out, nor did the sandals on your feet." What simple reminders of extraordinary care for ordinary concerns!

Question: Do you tend to look for God in exciting sea-crossings and overlook Him in enduring sandals?

Faithlift: Your feats as well as your feet concern your loving Father today. Walk in peace, knowing you're covered from top to toe.

FEBRUARY

FEBRUARY 1

Now what I am commanding you today is not too difficult for you or beyond your reach.
Deuteronomy 30:11

Further reading: Deuteronomy 30

How could God say this to a people whose ears were packed full of promises, blessings, commandments, and curses? How could God say this to His children who, through multiplied transgressions, trampled on God's grace, flirted with foreign gods, and toyed with pagan practices? God punctuated His decrees with the truth that they need not look to heaven or beyond the sea to locate God's words so they may obey. "No, the word is very near you; it is in your mouth and in your heart so you may obey it" (Deuteronomy 30:14). Lesser gods, powerless potentates, demand the impossible, the unthinkable. But the omnipotent God of Israel assigns to us what is not too difficult or beyond our reach. The difference is not in the portion assigned but in the power ascribed. God promises power to do what He prescribes. His commands are within reach because His power is within us.

Question: Are you worried about the commands or worshiping the Commander?

Faithlift: God's power within you makes obedience within your reach.

FEBRUARY 2

They are not just idle words for you—they are life.
Deuteronomy 32:47

Further reading: Deuteronomy 32

The lyrics of Moses' song hung on the Israelites like a

heavy cloak. The sweet song reminded them of God's faithfulness, protection, and grace-filled love. The words refreshed them like soft spring rain. But soon the softness was punctuated with thunderous reminders of the Israelites' disobedience. Their hearts sank when truth rained down in pelting sheets. Moses stood with Joshua, surveying his shivering sheep, and spoke sober words. "Take to heart all the words I have solemnly declared to you this day, so that you may command your children to obey carefully all the words of this law. They are not just idle words for you—they are your life" (Deuteronomy 32:46–47).

Words can pile up like yesterday's trash if we hear them but don't take them to heart. Only in our hearts do will, emotions, and the Spirit combine to produce true obedience. Real life flows from obeying God's words, not from merely hearing them.

Question: Do you have full ears but an empty heart?

Faithlift: Healthy hearts listen and obey.

FEBRUARY 3

As I was with Moses, so I will be with you; I will never leave you or forsake you. Joshua 1:5

Further reading: Joshua 1

These words contain both good and bad news. The good news is that God will never leave Joshua. The bad news is the "as I was with Moses" part. God's presence with Moses had not insulated Moses from trouble, suffering, and disappointment. God's presence had not kept Moses from disobedience and its consequences. That's the rub. God's presence doesn't guarantee our perfection. Joshua would make wise and unwise choices, as we do. But the good news is that God's love remains unflappable, reaching toward us despite our human imperfections. Joshua knew the honors of leadership were few and the hazards many. Joshua also knew that God had delivered His children from Egypt but not from individual choices and responsibilities. Even Moses, deliverer of God's children, had sustained scars. We sometimes expect God to protect us from poor choices and their consequences; thus, "as I was with Moses, so I will be with you" may come as bad news. Yet God's truth prevails to challenge and comfort: "I will never leave you or forsake you."

Question: Are you trusting in good news or in God?

Faithlift: God's love for you is unflappable; His presence unstoppable.

FEBRUARY 4

Have I not commanded you? Be strong and courageous. Do not be terrified; do not be discouraged, for the LORD *your God will be with you wherever you go.*
Joshua 1:9

Further reading: Joshua 1

How could God command Joshua to be strong and courageous? Can those traits be summoned on command? Would Joshua's knees settle down and his countenance lift by God's commands not to be terrified or discouraged? The strength and courage to succeed great Moses as leader of the unpredictable Israelites came, not through a chain of commands, but through a relationship with the Commander. Joshua's knees shook, his courage waned, his strength lagged, and he felt discouraged; but he found strength in the fact that God knew his weaknesses. If all-knowing God commanded strength, courage, fearlessness, and encouragement, then Joshua could face the knowns and unknowns that lay ahead.

Question: How well do you know the Commander?

Faithlift: God's presence gives perspective on today and tomorrow. He commands what He is capable of carrying out through your obedience.

FEBRUARY 5

. . . for the LORD your God is God in heaven above and on the earth below. Joshua 2:11

Further reading: Joshua 2

These are strange words coming from a harlot in a heathen culture! Rahab's reception of Joshua's spies was not rooted in her profession but in her awareness of a world beyond the walls of Jericho. As an innkeeper and prostitute she must have heard fearful whispers and brash denunciations of this foreign God and His miraculous deliverance of His children. While the other citizens of Jericho feared, Rahab formed her faith in the God of Israel. And so she risked her life to hide the spies, thus identifying herself with God's people. Such faith lifted Rahab to Faith's Hall of Fame in Hebrews 11:31, where we read, "By faith the prostitute Rahab, because she welcomed the spies, was not killed with those who were disobedient."

Question: How aware are you of God's work beyond the walls of your own culture?

Faithlift: That which prompts fear in others today may produce faith in you.

FEBRUARY 6

Consecrate yourselves, for tomorrow the LORD will do amazing things among you. Joshua 3:5

Further reading: Joshua 3

How sad if the only ones who ever received that promise were the children of Israel in Joshua's day! But God in His grace still performs amazing works among His children. If we fail to see God's miracles, it may be because we have not consecrated ourselves to God, and not because God lacks commitment to us. Consecration is total dedication of ourselves to God. Dedication commits us to a course of action, to a purpose. As long as we stay diffused, rushed, and spent, we will miss the mandate to consecrate ourselves and may find tomorrow as ordinary as today.

Question: Am I willing to narrow my focus and dedicate myself totally to God?

Faithlift: Consecration today prepares us for celebration tomorrow!

FEBRUARY 7

In the future, when your children ask you, "What do these stones mean?" tell them that the flow of the Jordan was cut off before the ark of the covenant of the LORD. *When it crossed the Jordan, the waters of the Jordan were cut off. These stones are to be a memorial to the people of Israel forever.*
Joshua 4:6–7

Further reading: Joshua 3–4

Years earlier, the Red Sea had parted and Moses had led the children of Israel through walls of water until they stepped onto the sand of Shur. Now Moses was dead, and his successor, Joshua, needed assurance of God's presence and power to lead the Israelites. So God rolled up the Jordan like a liquid scroll, and they all marched across on dry ground. Afterward, God asked Joshua to choose a representative from each of the twelve tribes to carry a stone from the middle of the Jordan River to the Israelites' campsite. These stones were not religious relics or souvenirs but reminders of God's faithfulness and protection. The stones said that God's presence and power had passed on from Moses to Joshua. The significance of the stones was to be passed down from generation to generation. These river rocks were not simply for display, as in some geological exhibit. They were to be topics of conversation, visual reminders of the power of invisible Jehovah God.

Collecting teacups, stamps, coins, dolls, antiques, and baseball cards, to name a few, interests numbers of old and young people in our culture. We would do well to gather some stones of significance for those who come after us, some rock-solid reminders of God's faithfulness. Our children and other seekers of God would fare better with a few stones than with shelves of this world's collectibles.

Question: What are you collecting?

Faithlift: Begin collecting stones for storytelling and pass on an imperishable, tax-free inheritance.

FEBRUARY 8

But the Israelites acted unfaithfully in regard to the devoted things. Joshua 7:1

Further reading: Joshua 7

God clearly instructed His children to "keep away from the devoted things, so that [they would] not bring about [their] own destruction. . . . All the silver and gold and the articles of bronze and iron [were] sacred to the LORD and must go into his treasury" (Joshua 6:18, 19). Achan, however, took exception to God's command, valuing the goods more than obedience. "When I saw in the plunder a beautiful robe from Babylonia, two hundred shekels of silver and a wedge of gold weighing fifty shekels, I coveted them and took them. They are hidden in the ground inside my tent, with the silver underneath" (Joshua 7:21). That which was coveted in private and collected in secret brought public and personal consequences. The Israelites were routed in battle, and later Achan and his family were destroyed along with all his possessions.

Question: Are you faithfully obeying or frantically obtaining?

Faithlift: True treasure is found in a focus on God, not goods.

FEBRUARY 9

The men of Israel sampled their provisions but did not inquire of the LORD. Joshua 9:14

Further reading: Joshua 9

Fear spread like a destructive plague to the godless kingdoms surrounding the Israelites. Battle statistics boldly communicated an ongoing saga of victories for the visitors and slaughter for the home team. The Gibeonites decided to prevent the visiting Israelites from chalking up another victory. They dressed and acted as though they were from far away, knowing full well that the Israelites were to destroy the current dwellers in the Promised Land. "They went as a delegation whose donkeys were loaded with worn-out sacks and old wineskins, cracked and mended. The men put worn and patched sandals on their feet and wore old clothes. All the bread of their food supply was dry and moldy. Then they went to Joshua . . . and the men of Israel, 'We have come from a distant country; make a treaty with us'" (vv. 4–6). Joshua and the men of Israel questioned them to see if they were from the surrounding area, but the Gibeonites said, "This bread of ours was warm when we packed it at home on the day we left to come to you. But now see how dry and moldy it is" (v. 12). Joshua and the Israelite men fell for the ruse. "[They] sampled their provisions but did not inquire of the LORD" (v. 14). Joshua then ignorantly signed a treaty with those he had been commanded to destroy.

Question: On what basis will you make choices today?

Faithlift: God will never trick those who put their trust in Him.

FEBRUARY 10

After that whole generation had been gathered to their fathers, another generation grew up, who knew neither the LORD nor what he had done for Israel. Judges 2:10

Further reading: Judges 2

Handing down faith from one generation to the next, from parent to child, from older to younger, is God's pattern for relaying truth. In a few years God's much-loved children failed to pass on the principles of holy living to their children. Somehow, they communicated that following God was less significant than blending in to a new culture. Did the older ones model preoccupation with settling in, plucking grapes they had not planted, drawing water from wells they had not dug, enjoying cities they had not built, sorting through goodies they had inherited? Subtly, choice by choice, tiny but tangible gods replaced the God of their fathers and mothers. And now a fresh generation stood knee-deep in grapes, but empty of gratitude to the God who had brought them from Egypt and had given them everything they now enjoyed. Focused on the duties and delicacies of the day, they forgot their Deliverer.

Question: What will the next generation learn about God from you?

Faithlift: God is committed to helping you communicate His truths to the next generation.

FEBRUARY 11

The LORD is with you, mighty warrior. Judges 6:12

Further reading: Judges 6

Gideon was neither the picture of a farmer nor a mighty warrior as he threshed wheat in a winepress one ordinary day. God's label, "mighty warrior," seemed as inappropriate on Gideon as a king's armor on a young boy named David. Gideon, however, did not focus on the adulation but on God's seeming absence. "But sir, . . . if the LORD is with us, why has all this happened to us?" (v. 13). God didn't budge when Gideon balked. He told gentle Gideon, "Go in the strength you have" (v. 14). In humility Gideon reiterated the inappropriateness of God's call to him to save Israel. When he looked at himself, he recalled, "I am the least in my family" (v. 15). But God replied, "I will be with you, and you will strike down the Midianites as if they were but one man" (v. 16). God with one weak but willing man is always more than enough for any Midianites.

Question: Do you rely more on God's call or on your own characteristics?

Faithlift: God and you are a majority to handle your Midianites today.

FEBRUARY 12

When Gideon heard the dream and its interpretation, he worshiped God. Judges 7:15

Further reading: Judges 7

Gideon, like most of us, needed a lot of reassurance that God had picked the right person and would perform what He had promised: "Get up, go down against the camp, because I am going to give it into your hands" (v. 9). Gideon was unaccustomed to God's call or to great challenges. So God not only spoke to Gideon, but He also told him to go down to the enemy camp and listen in on their conversation. Now this was no small enemy encampment. "The Midianites, the Amalekites and all the other eastern peoples had settled in the valley, thick as locusts. Their camels could no more be counted than the sand on the seashore" (v. 12). Gideon and his servant showed up, ears strained, "just as a man was telling a friend his dream" (v. 13). The dream's interpretation meant, according to the enemy, that God had given the Midianites and the whole camp into Gideon's hands. When Gideon overheard this conversation, he worshiped God, then he fled back to the camp of Israel and shouted, "Get up! The LORD has given the Midianite camp into your hands" (v. 15). In his excitement, Gideon still remembered to worship God.

Question: Do you remember to give credit to God and worship the One who makes your victories possible today?

Faithlift: There's joy in bowing to worship before beginning your work.

FEBRUARY 13

But Gideon told them, "I will not rule over you, nor will my son rule over you. The LORD will rule over you." Judges 8:23

Further reading: Judges 8

Gideon's ears were ringing with praise from the Israelites. He was their hero—he had saved them from the Midianites. The people pushed to give Gideon a swift promotion. Gideon must have been tempted to shift from hoeing wheat to ruling tribes, but he communicated a definite no. This was not a no needing a few more fringe benefits to twist it to a yes. Gideon's choice was rooted in true humility. Praise had not blurred his perspective on himself or on God. He knew the true hero, and it wasn't a guy named Gideon. It took greatness of character to turn the focus from Gideon to God.

Question: How do you handle praise?

Faithlift: The more we know God, the freer we are to give Him the praise.

FEBRUARY 14

O LORD, I beg you, let the man of God you sent to us come again to teach us how to bring up the boy who is to be born. Judges 13:8

Further reading: Judges 13

What joy when this childless couple learned that they were going to have a baby! When reality nudged their minds as the initial news had hugged their hearts, they prayed to God for help. While they were novices with a newborn, they were seasoned in matters of the spirit, so they did the usual and called on their Father for advice. God didn't answer all their questions, but He gave a demonstration of the force behind the facts. And we read, "The woman gave birth to a boy and named him Samson. He grew and the LORD blessed him" (Judges 13:24).

Question: When you are concerned, do you naturally call on your Father for advice?

Faithlift: Faith sees the power behind the facts.

FEBRUARY 15

But [Samson] did not know that the LORD had left him.
Judges 16:20

Further reading: Judges 16:1–22

Nagging Delilah eventually prodded the truth from Samson. "I have been a Nazirite set apart to God since birth. If my head were shaved, my strength would leave me, and I would become as weak as any other man" (v. 17). So, while Samson slept, Delilah shaved, and he awoke minus more than hair. What a sad picture! Short-haired Samson, ready to take on the Philistines, as usual, but unaware that this time he would go in his own strength. Mighty Samson, minus God's Spirit, was powerless against the Philistines. They blinded his eyes and bound him with bronze shackles and set him grinding like an animal. Samson, tortured in body and spirit, crushed grain instead of Philistines, and plodded in small circles like a malfunctioning machine.

Question: In whose strength do you go today?

Faithlift: When Samson cried, "O Sovereign LORD, remember me" (Judges 16:28), God remembered. When you cry for His strength today, He will remember you, as well.

FEBRUARY 16

So the two women went on until they came to Bethlehem.
Ruth 1:19

Further reading: Ruth 1

The book of Ruth is a thrilling story of God's love. Ruth, Naomi's daughter-in-law, made a commitment to leave her family and the familiar surroundings of Moab and move on to the unknowns of Bethlehem with her mother-in-law, Naomi. Ruth's commitment, "Where you go I will go, and where you stay I will stay. Your people will be my people and your God my God" (v. 16), has inspired love songs and lovers for centuries. More important, however, such commitment moved Ruth and moves us toward Bethlehem. Once there, we will meet our Savior in ways we never can if we remain in our Moabs surrounded by faithless, familiar security.

Question: Am I willing to leave my Moab-like place of security to move on to Bethlehem?

Faithlift: Faith is a daily trek from Moab to the Messiah.

FEBRUARY 17

I went away full, but the LORD has brought me back empty. Ruth 1:21

Further reading: Ruth 1

Naomi, mourning the loss of her husband and two sons, must not have been the best traveling companion for Ruth. As she entered her old town and met old friends, she poured out tales of emptiness and affliction, never once adding a "but Ruth." True, her losses were staggering, but she was not totally empty. Naomi had Ruth! Yet God gives us a hint of good to come. "[They arrived] in Bethlehem as the barley harvest was beginning" (v. 22). Life had seemed full to Naomi years earlier when she had packed up her household and headed to Moab with her husband and sons. Life looked empty now as she reentered her hometown minus everything she had left with earlier. But Naomi and Ruth were about to receive more than barley in Bethlehem. The all-powerful God that Ruth had heard about in Moab would make Himself known to two powerless people who had committed to go the Bethlehem way.

Question: What standard do you use to determine if you are full or empty?

Faithlift: There's more than barley in Bethlehem; there's living bread and water.

FEBRUARY 18

[Boaz said to Ruth,] "May the L*ORD repay you for what you have done. May you be richly rewarded by the* L*ORD, the God of Israel, under whose wings you have come to take refuge." Ruth 2:12*

Further reading: Ruth 2

No banners or bands welcomed Ruth when she arrived in Bethlehem. She had forsaken her familiar gods for the true God of Israel while living in Moab, for Naomi and her family must have reiterated God's miracles for His children. Yet, as a newcomer to faith and to fields of barley, Ruth found no manna or quail to feed her hunger, only fields to comb for small pickings. But Ruth did not glean unnoticed in a barley field in Bethlehem. God noticed her fresh faith in Him, her committed love for Naomi, and her willingness to glean instead of grumble, so He touched the heart of Boaz, who owned the field. How Boaz must have encouraged Ruth with his kindness and keen observations! God's wings, place of refuge for Ruth, hovered over Bethlehem, stirring up a harvest of blessings for an old and a young believer.

Question: Will you believe that God sees you in your barley field, your place of difficult duty?

Faithlift: God's blessings crop up even in barley fields!

FEBRUARY 19

So Boaz took Ruth and she became his wife. And the L*ORD enabled her to conceive, and she gave birth to a son. The women said to Naomi: "Praise be to the* L*ORD, who this day has not left you without a kinsman-redeemer. May he become famous throughout Israel!" Ruth 4:13–14*

Further reading: Ruth 4

What a love story! What full hearts for empty-handed Ruth and Naomi! Not long ago they had entered Bethlehem's borders as two homeless, battered-by-circumstances women. Now they had status in the community, security, and a baby boy named Obed. What a harvest! The women of the town huddled around Naomi, an old woman with young life in her lap and fresh hope in her heart. They exclaimed, "He will renew your life and sustain you in your old age. For your daughter-in-law, who loves you and who is better to you than seven sons, has given him birth" (v. 15). Ruth's simple but tough choices to love and obey readied the soil for an abundant harvest.

Question: How are you tending the soil of your heart?

Faithlift: Obedience plows, love nourishes, and God produces a harvest of blessing in our barley fields.

FEBRUARY 20

And they named him Obed. He was the father of Jesse, the father of David. Ruth 4:17

Further reading: Ruth 4:17

This small verse is packed with encouragement for people with a past. Many people, non-believers included, know of David. Some have heard of Ruth and Naomi. Still fewer know of Obed. It is easy to race right over a genealogy to get to the good stuff—something with hope and application to us today. Well, great news is packed in this list of begats. Ruth, from a pagan culture, married into a good Jewish family. Her husband, one of Naomi's sons, had died in Moab, but still she committed to move to Bethlehem with her widowed mother-in-law, Naomi. In a barley field she met the owner, Boaz, and later married him. The incredible encouragement is that Boaz' mother was Rahab the harlot—a person with a past, until God "Rahab"-bilitated her. She must have taught her son thoughtful ways to relate to women, for Boaz was known for his kindness. Ruth and Boaz had a son named Obed, of whom the women of Bethlehem said, "May he become famous throughout Israel!" (v. 14). Little did they know! Note these excerpts from Matthew 1 on the genealogy of Jesus Christ: "Salmon the father of Boaz, whose mother was Rahab, Boaz the father of Obed, whose mother was Ruth, Obed the father of Jesse, and Jesse the father of King David (vv. 5, 6) . . . and Jacob the father of Joseph, the husband of Mary, of whom was born Jesus, who is called Christ" (v. 16). God not only provided a way for two pagan women, Ruth and Rahab, to become believers and to be adopted into His family; God chose them to be part of His Son's earthly genealogy.

Question: Where is God "Rahab"-bilitating your life?

Faithlift: You come from a great family! May people notice your resemblance to your Father today!

FEBRUARY 21

[Elkanah] had two wives; one was called Hannah and the other Peninnah. Peninnah had children, but Hannah had none.
1 Samuel 1:2

Further reading: 1 Samuel 1:1–18

It is painful when the haves and have-nots share the same space. In that culture it was a disgrace to be childless, like Hannah. Elkanah loved Hannah and tried his best to show her, but her pain persisted. Peninnah "kept provoking her in order to irritate her. This went on year after year" (vv. 6, 7). Hannah's pain hung in day after day, year after year. There is a sorrow that is rooted in our own wrong choices, but Hannah's sorrows came from circumstances beyond her control. So Hannah prayed. But even in her prayer she was misunderstood by Eli, the priest. "As she kept on praying to the LORD, Eli observed her mouth. Hannah was praying in her heart, and her lips were moving but her voice was not heard. Eli thought she was drunk" (vv. 12–13). Hannah humbly distinguished intoxication from intercession for the elderly priest, who then blessed his broken parishioner. "Go in peace, and may the God of Israel grant you what you have asked of him" (v. 17). And God did just that!

Question: How do you respond when grossly misunderstood?

Faithlift: You can trust God with your broken heart.

FEBRUARY 22

Then she went her way and ate something, and her face was no longer downcast. 1 Samuel 1:18

Further reading: 1 Samuel 1

Before Hannah's circumstances changed, her countenance lifted. That's faith! She believed when she didn't see anything different from the day before. Hannah still had to walk home from the temple with Peninnah and her brood—vocal and visual reminders that nothing had changed externally for Hannah. But internally, while empty of child, she was full of faith which showed in her actions. Hannah got up, ate, and looked like she had a wonderful secret. "Early the next morning they arose and worshiped before the LORD and then went back to their home at Ramah" (v. 19). Hannah, barren in body but not in spirit, stopped weeping and began worshiping. "And the LORD remembered her. So in the course of time Hannah conceived and gave birth to a son" (vv. 19–20).

Question: What does my countenance reveal about my faith?

Faithlift: When our emptiness, like Hannah's, sends us to God, we never return barren.

FEBRUARY 23

Eli's sons were wicked men; they had no regard for the LORD. 1 Samuel 2:12

Further reading: 1 Samuel 2

Before Hannah knew she was going to have a baby, she promised God that if she had a son, she would give him to the Lord. It is one thing to make a promise when you are empty. It is quite another matter to keep your promise when full. Mothering made the years slip by quickly, and soon Samuel was weaned and ready to be brought to the temple. Hannah faced a tough challenge of faith as she prepared to permanently drop off her son at Eli's—Day and Night Care Center. Eli's wicked sons had marred his reputation as a father. How could she leave her precious Samuel with such a family? The answer was in God! God would tend to her son. She had promised her son to God, not to Eli. She must have left Samuel's ears ringing with the sounds of his mother worshiping, not weeping. Read Hannah's prayer in 1 Samuel 2:1–10 and take note of her view of God. Such a God would care for her son.

Question: Do those closest to you catch your fear or your faith?

Faithlift: Fear and faith are both contagious. Spread faith today.

FEBRUARY 24

Meanwhile, the boy Samuel grew up in the presence of the LORD. 1 Samuel 2:21

Further reading: 1 Samuel 2

This verse communicates that Hannah's trust in God was well placed. In verse 26 we read, "And the boy Samuel continued to grow in stature and in favor with the LORD and with men." Hannah grew, too. Each year she brought her son a new coat "when she went up with her husband to offer the annual sacrifice" (v. 19). While she stitched his cloaks, she must have blitzed heaven with prayers for Samuel, and praying has a way of growing a person. The visible cloaks were insignificant compared to the invisible prayer coverings that blanketed Samuel. What a wise mother!

Question: Where is my focus: the clothes closet or the prayer closet?

Faithlift: Cover someone with your prayers today.

FEBRUARY 25

[The elders of Israel] said to [Samuel], "You are old, and your sons do not walk in your ways; now appoint a king to lead us, such as all the other nations have." 1 Samuel 8:5

Further reading: 1 Samuel 8

Samuel was confronted with two of life's toughest disappointments: failure as a parent (his sons did not walk in God's ways) and failure as a leader (the people wanted a king). How did Samuel respond? "He prayed to the LORD" (v. 6). Scripture does not list Samuel's grievances against these elders, God, or his sons. Neither did he bury himself in guilt. Samuel, birthed and covered in prayer, called naturally to his Father God, who gave him perspective on His children and Samuel's. "It is not you they have rejected as their king, but me." While elders and youngsters whined for a king, old Samuel went to the Lord and found perspective as a parent and comfort as a child.

Question: How do you respond to disappointment and failure?

Faithlift: Pressure responds to prayer.

FEBRUARY 26

Go and look for the donkeys. 1 Samuel 9:3

Further reading: 1 Samuel 9

Saul, tall and handsome son of Kish, lumbered off with a servant to comb the Judean hills for his father's lost donkeys. After a couple of fruitless days, Saul was ready to head home. By now, he figured, his dad would be more concerned about his whereabouts than about the animals. But the servant persuaded Saul to persevere and seek the prophet in town. Through the prophet Samuel, Saul located his father's donkeys and learned that God had chosen him as Israel's first king. What a dramatic shift—from searching for donkeys to serving as king!

Question: How do I view days of seeming futility?

Faithlift: Expect God to surprise you, whether tending donkeys or dynasties.

FEBRUARY 27

This is the man the Lord has chosen as your king. There isn't his equal in all of Israel!
1 Samuel 10:24, The Living Bible

Further reading: 1 Samuel 10

The leap from tending donkeys to taking on a kingship seemed too much for young Saul. When the time came for the leaders to present Saul as king, he was nowhere to be found. When they inquired of the Lord, God told them, "He has hidden himself among the baggage" (v. 22). What strange behavior for God's hand-picked first king of Israel! Couldn't God have found someone with more self-confidence, a born leader? Stranger than Saul's ways were Samuel's words: "This is the man the Lord has chosen as your king. There isn't his equal in all of Israel!" While Saul, the chosen, sought a hiding place, God, the chooser, sought a humble man and then stood by His choice!

Question: How are you responding to God's challenges? Are you hiding in the baggage of your life?

Faithlift: God sees through your baggage and lifts you up and declares, "There is not your equal!"

FEBRUARY 28

But Saul kept silent.
1 Samuel 10:27

Further reading: 1 Samuel 10

Saul, like most leaders, had his supporters and his enemies. God's declaration concerning this young king fell on some unimpressed ears. While Saul and a few "valiant men whose hearts God had touched" (v. 26) traveled to his home in Gibeah, others despised him. "Some troublemakers said, 'How can this fellow save us?' They despised him and brought him no gifts" (v. 27). Saul, fresh from hiding in the baggage and from hearing God's words of affirmation through Samuel, neither retaliated in frustration nor retreated in fear. He simply kept quiet.

Question: How do you respond to those who try to erase God's words of affirmation and purpose to you?

Faithlift: You have the right and privilege to remain silent.

FEBRUARY 29

I have been your leader from my youth until this day. Here I stand. Testify against me in the presence of the LORD and his anointed. 1 Samuel 12:2–3

Further reading: 1 Samuel 12

Samuel, bent with age, stood tall as Israel's outgoing leader. He challenged the people to list any bribes and cite any oppressions by his hand. There were none. Remember, this man had not just squeaked through a four-year term of office. He had been God's man since he was a boy, decade after decade, until this day when Saul was confirmed as Israel's first king. Samuel's integrity was impeccable. "'You have not cheated or oppressed us,' they replied. 'You have not taken anything from anyone's hand'"(v. 4). What a tribute to Samuel and his God. Samuel stood as God's servant-leader.

Question: What choices do you face today that challenge your integrity?

Faithlift: God's strength and wisdom equip you to stand tall as a true servant-leader.

MARCH

MARCH 1

Pray to the LORD *your God for your servants so that we will not die, for we have added to all our other sins the evil of asking for a king. 1 Samuel 12:19*

Further reading: 1 Samuel 12

Samuel's farewell address hung like crepe over God's children. Once again God had created a word picture of His faithfulness as their Father and of their forgetfulness as His children. Like a living computer, aged Samuel gave verbal printouts of their rebellion against God, including demanding a king when the Lord was their King. Suddenly, truth pelted their hearts and sent shivers through these frightened sheep. A sense of alienation crowded in behind fear; and God's much-loved sheep crouched behind Samuel, begging him to pray to his God on their behalf. How swift the turn from fearlessly demanding a king to fearfully pleading for their lives. How subtle the shift from *our God* to *your God.*

Question: Do your demands show a shift away from God as King?

Faithlift: Though you may feel alienated from God, He is near enough to hear your faintest cry.

MARCH 2

As for me, far be it from me that I should sin against the LORD *by failing to pray for you.
1 Samuel 12:23*

Further reading: 1 Samuel 12

This was Samuel's opportunity of a lifetime. The people cowered before him, pleading with Samuel to pray for them. He could retaliate for swapping him for a king by refusing to budge another inch on their behalf. But Samuel's heart, like Moses' and Joshua's before him, beat to the Father's rhythm. He moved beyond what the people requested of him to what his God required. "Far be it from me that I should sin against the LORD by failing to pray for you. And I will teach you the way that is good and right" (v. 23). Instead of chastising them, Samuel agreed to intercede for and instruct them.

Question: How are you responding to the difficult people in your life?

Faithlift: Synchronize your heart with the Father's and find grace for the difficult people in your life today.

MARCH 3

When Samuel reached him, Saul said, "The LORD bless you! I have carried out the LORD's instructions." 1 Samuel 15:13

Further reading: 1 Samuel 15

What strange words from King Saul! God's commands were to totally destroy all Amalekites and everything that belonged to them. But Saul and his army spared Agag and the best sheep, cattle, the fat calves and lambs and everything that was good. Saul's self-righteous words, "I have carried out the Lord's instructions," punctuated the air that was already full of sounds and smells of Amalekite animals. Samuel, old but not deaf, asked, "What then is this bleating of sheep in my ears" (v. 14)? Saul muttered, "The soldiers brought them from the Amalekites; they spared the best of the sheep and cattle to sacrifice to the LORD your God" (v. 15). Samuel simply cried, "Stop!" (v. 16).

Question: What good things have you hidden under false pretenses?

Faithlift: Obedience needs no excuses.

MARCH 4

But Samuel replied: "Does the LORD delight in burnt offerings and sacrifices as much as in obeying the voice of the LORD?"
1 Samuel 15:22a

Further reading: 1 Samuel 15

Self-deception was not unique to King Saul. It is tempting to manipulate our desires as if they were God's. There were times when God gave the plunder to the soldiers, but not this time. The instructions were clear: "Destroy everything" (15:3). The soldiers didn't go after everything with uncritical abandon. They focused on the best of everything. And when in doubt concerning God's clear directions, they called their plunder a sacrifice to the Lord God. But Samuel's response jerked them from their twisted, selfish interpretations of God's strong decrees. He honed in on the heart of the matter: "To obey is better than sacrifice" (v. 22).

Question: Is there a place where you are sacrificing rather than obeying?

Faithlift: Our obedience gives joy to God.

MARCH 5

Then Saul said to Samuel, "I have sinned. I violated the LORD's command and your instructions. I was afraid of the people and so I gave in to them."
1 Samuel 15:24

Further reading: 1 Samuel 15

Fear motivates. Saul began his kingship hiding in the baggage (see 1 Samuel 10:22), and he forfeited his kingship because the wrong fears ruled him. Because Saul feared man, not God, he offered the burnt offering that Samuel was to make (see 1 Samuel 13:7–14). Because Saul feared the Philistines, not God, he called for a medium to bring up Samuel (see 1 Samuel 28:5–11). Saul also feared David. But David refused the opportunity to take Saul's life out of fear of the Lord. "The LORD forbid that I should do such a thing to my master, the LORD's anointed, or lift my hand against him; for he is the anointed of the LORD" (1 Samuel 24:6). While tall Saul and his armies cowered before Goliath, young David feared God and felled the giant (see 1 Samuel 17). Saul, ruled by the wrong fears, spent his years retreating, retaliating, and recoiling instead of ruling as God had planned.

Question: What role does fear play in ordering your actions?

Faithlift: Fear the Lord and your giants will fall at your feet.

MARCH 6

The LORD said to Samuel, "How long will you mourn for Saul, since I have rejected him as king over Israel?" 1 Samuel 16:1

Further reading: 1 Samuel 15:34–16:3

Samuel must have felt like a father to Saul. Several times we read how difficult it was for Samuel to speak God's hard truths to Saul. When God told Samuel that Saul had disobeyed His command to destroy the Amalekites and everything that belonged to them, we learn that "Samuel was troubled, and he cried out to the LORD all that night" (1 Samuel 15:11). After Samuel spoke God's words to Saul, he left for his home in Ramah and Saul headed to Gibeah. But "until the day Samuel died, he did not go to see Saul again, though Samuel mourned for him. And the LORD was grieved that he had made Saul king over Israel" (1 Samuel 15:35). Saul was like a son to Samuel, and so Samuel mourned over his reckless ways. But the time came when God said "Enough!" God's purposes for Samuel did not include spending his last days mourning for Saul and what might have been. And so His words to Samuel were direct: "Fill your horn with oil and be on your way; I am sending you to Jesse of Bethlehem. I have chosen one of his sons to be king" (1 Samuel 16:1). Samuel did what he had done since he was a small boy: he obeyed the Lord.

Question: Are you mourning over what might have been instead of obeying and enjoying what God has planned for you today?

Faithlift: Don't let your mourning cloud God's plans for you.

MARCH 7

[Samuel] asked Jesse, "Are these all the sons you have?" "There is still the youngest," Jesse answered, "but he is tending the sheep." 1 Samuel 16:11

Further reading: 1 Samuel 16:1–13

After consecrating Jesse and his sons, Samuel invited them to the sacrifice. Samuel thought he'd struck gold when he met Jesse's eldest son, Eliab. But God whispered powerful guidance in Samuel's old ears. "Do not consider his appearance or his height, for I have rejected him. The LORD does not look at the things man looks at. Man looks at the outward appearance, but the LORD looks at the heart" (v. 7). Then six more sons paraded before Samuel, but none resonated with God's Spirit in Samuel. So Samuel inquired of Jesse, "Are these all the sons you have?" Learning that there was one more, a young shepherd, they sat and waited until Jesse's youngest son arrived. Samuel looked and listened and heard, "Rise and anoint him; he is the one" (v. 12). And David, the unlikely, became David, the anointed.

Question: Do you have yourself or another in a box marked "unlikely"?

Faithlift: Don't be resigned; rejoice in the God who redeems the unlikely.

MARCH 8

[After David heard Goliath shout his usual defiance, he asked the soldiers nearby,] "Who is this uncircumcised Philistine that he

should defy the armies of the living God?" 1 Samuel 17:26

Further reading: 1 Samuel 17: 1–37

David shuttled between Bethlehem, where he tended his father's sheep, and the Valley of Elah, where the men of Israel were fighting against the Philistines. On this day Jesse had sent David with a care package from home: cheeses, roasted grain, and bread for his brothers and their commander. David arrived just in time to hear Goliath, more than nine feet tall, challenge the Israelites to send one man to fight him. The winner would take all. David heard the giant's rantings and saw Israel's army retreat in fear. Like Joshua and Caleb (see Numbers 13 and 14), David was not intimidated by giants. The giant's statistics paled beside David's God. So, less from teen-age bravado than from belief in God, he courageously presented himself to King Saul and said, "Let no one lose heart on account of this Philistine; your servant will go and fight him" (1 Samuel 17:32). David's confidence in God melted the giant to a mere man.

Question: Are you facing your giants with fear or with faith?

Faithlift: God is more than a match for any giants you face today.

MARCH 9

"I cannot go in there," he said to Saul, "because I am not used to them." 1 Samuel 17:39

Further reading: 1 Samuel 17

Saul must have felt rebuked by this courageous young man who was willing to take on Saul's giant. How the soldiers must have snickered at the youth's brazenness! But eventually Saul said, "Go and the LORD be with you" (v. 37). Saul even went so far as to remove his own tunic, coat of armor, bronze helmet, and sword and give them to David for protection. How awkward he must have looked, stumbling around in tall Saul's armor. But David's confidence rested neither in Saul's armor nor his army. David trusted God and the familiar defenses of a shepherd. "Then he took his staff in his hand, chose five smooth stones from the stream, put them in the pouch of his shepherd's bag and, with his sling in his hand, approached the Philistine" (v. 40). All snickering must have stopped as the men of Israel watched their seemingly unprotected replacement approach the giant. But David had all he needed: faith in God and five smooth stones.

Question: Is your confidence in someone else's armor?

Faithlift: God and your five smooth stones are more than sufficient to handle your giants.

MARCH 10

The LORD forbid that I should do such a thing to my master, the LORD's anointed, or lift my hand against him; for he is the anointed of the LORD.
1 Samuel 24:6

Further reading: 1 Samuel 24

As David's popularity with the people rose, Saul's fear and animosity toward him increased. Jealousy fueled Saul's rage and threatened David's life numerous times. So David, God's anointed and Saul's true friend, became an outlaw, and "all those who were in distress or in debt or discontented gathered around him, and he became their leader. About four hundred men were with him" (1 Samuel 22:2). One day Saul learned of David's whereabouts and took three thousand men to capture him. At a cave Saul "went in to relieve himself. David and his men were far back in the cave" (1 Samuel 24:3). David's men urged him to see this as the time when God had said, "I will give your enemy into your hands for you to deal with as you wish" (v. 4). But David didn't see it as an opportunity to kill but as a chance to show kindness to his master, God's anointed one. So David merely "crept up unnoticed and cut off a corner of Saul's robe" (v. 4), like leaving a business card. Hear Saul's response to David's kindness: "May the LORD reward you well for the way you treated me today" (v. 19). And He did!

Question: Who is your Saul? How are you treating him or her?

Faithlift: Trust your Sauls to God, and He will reward you.

MARCH 11

She was an intelligent and beautiful woman, but her husband, a Calebite, was surly and mean in his dealings. 1 Samuel 25:3

Further reading: 1 Samuel 25

The story of Abigail and Nabal intrigues more than incurable romantics. Nabal— ungrateful, inhospitable, selfish, rude, and foolish—contrasts starkly with his wife Abigail, who was beautiful, intelligent, respected, and godly. One day, during sheep shearing time, Abigail faced an extraordinary challenge. David and his men provided a band of protection around Nabal's shepherds and sheep. It was customary to be hospitable to these unpaid protectors, so David was not out of line when he sent ten of his young men to greet Nabal and ask him to "give [his] servants and [his] son David whatever [he could] find for them" (v. 8). Nabal responded with self-centered ingratitude. "Why should I take my bread and water, and the meat I have slaughtered for my shearers, and give it to men coming from who knows where?" (v. 11). David's men returned empty-handed to report Nabal's harsh words. David responded, "Put on your swords!" (v. 13). But one of Nabal's servants reported to Abigail, our master "hurled insults at them. Yet these men were very good to us . . . . Night and day they were a wall around us . . . . Now think it over and see what you can do, because disaster is hanging over our master and his whole household. He is such a wicked man that no one can talk to him" (vv. 14–17). And respected, godly, wise Abigail "lost no time" (v. 18).

Question: Do those who work with you see you more as a Nabal or an Abigail?

Faithlift: Prepare a feast of encouragement for hungry hearts around you.

MARCH 12

Praise be to the LORD, the God of Israel, who has sent you today to meet me. May you be blessed for your good judgment. 1 Samuel 25:32

Further reading: 1 Samuel 25

David knew that God had sent Abigail to stay his hand from justified but needless bloodshed. God used Abigail to give David perspective and to remind him of his greater call and purpose in life. "When the LORD has done for my master every good thing he promised concerning him and has appointed him leader over Israel, my master will not have on his conscience the staggering burden of needless bloodshed or of having avenged himself" (v. 30–31). Abigail's words rang true. How easy for David to lose that sense of mission while hiding out with a ragtag band of outlaws and malcontents! (See 1 Samuel 22:2.) How wise of Abigail to remind David that she knew God had chosen him to be king. Why blow his high calling by stooping to destroy Nabal? Her words stayed David's hand and prompted praise to God and blessing for Abigail.

Question: Who needs words of encouragement from you today?

Faithlift: God's wisdom encouraged well-drawn conclusions, not quick-drawn swords.

MARCH 13

Then David accepted from her hand what she had brought him and said, "Go home in peace. I have heard your words and granted your request." 1 Samuel 25:35

Further reading: 1 Samuel 25

Abigail's words cut clean through peripheral issues of vengeance and damaged egos. But David had to choose whether to act on his feelings or on Abigail's wisdom. He chose to heed her words and hold his sword. He would rely on His great God to deal with small Nabal. "About ten days later, the LORD struck Nabal and he died" (v. 38). So David accepted her feast for his hungry men and extended peace to Abigail's hungry heart. After Nabal's death, David sent for wise Abigail to become his wife. In a matter of days Abigail went from being married to a mean man named Nabal to being the wife of God's main man, David.

Question: How well do you accept what God gives you through another person?

Faithlift: God is able to handle your Nabal!

MARCH 14

When Abigail saw David . . . she fell at his feet and said: "My lord, let the blame be on me alone." 1 Samuel 25:23–24

Further reading: 1 Samuel 25

How humiliating to be married to a Nabal! How easy to let him get what he deserved from David's hands! But Abigail knew that Nabal's rude behavior would bring rash consequences for all the men who belonged to him and consequences for David, as well. Nabal refused to let David and his men come to the sheep-shearing feast, so Abigail prepared to bring the feast to them. She brought "two hundred loaves of bread, two skins of wine, five dressed sheep, five seahs [about one bushel] of roasted grain, a hundred cakes of raisins and two hundred cakes of pressed figs" (v. 18). But food alone could not have satisfied David. Abigail brought greater gifts: wisdom, humility, integrity, and perspective. She did not cover up or excuse Nabal's behavior: "May my lord pay no attention to that wicked man Nabal. He is just like his name—his name is Fool, and folly goes with him" (v. 25). But her discreet, wise preparation of the feast, her presentation of Nabal's folly, and her wise words provided a covering for Nabal, for her household, and for David and his men.

Question: How are you dealing with the Nabals in your life?

Faithlift: Love covers without covering up.

MARCH 15

David replied, "No, my brothers, you must not do that with what the LORD has given us."
1 Samuel 30:23

Further reading: 1 Samuel 30

David and his army of six hundred men began pursuing the Amalekites, who had attacked and burned their home, Ziklag, and carried off their women and children. When they reached the Besor Ravine, two hundred men stayed behind, too exhausted to continue. David went ahead with the four hundred and recovered all the Amalekites had taken—people and possessions, plus "plunder of the LORD's enemies" (v. 26). "But all the evil men and troublemakers among David's followers said, 'Because they [the two hundred] did not go out with us, we will not share with them the plunder we recovered. However, each man may take his wife and children and go" (v. 22). David, perhaps learning from his wife, Abigail, reminded the troublemakers that they were brothers and that whatever they had came from the Lord. Therefore, "the share of the man who stayed with the supplies [was] to be the same as that of him who went down to the battle. All [would] share alike" (v. 24). This principle still applies in the military.

Question: Who needs a share of what God has given to you?

Faithlift: The antidote for selfishness is sharing.

MARCH 16

David was thirty years old when he became king. 2 Samuel 5:4

Further reading: 2 Samuel 5:1–5

Many years elapsed between the day Samuel anointed young David's head in Bethlehem (see 1 Samuel 16) and the day the tribes of Israel gathered at Hebron to anoint David king of Israel. How many times he must have wondered if he would really reign. What did he do when patience waned, when others provoked him? Did his wife Abigail temper him, did psalms from his sheep-tending years etch deep truths into his thoughts? Did the old melodies and memories of quiet times with God hug his heart until the truths of God calmed his spirit or energized him for the latest challenge? During the waiting and faith-stretching years, did David sing, "Wait for the LORD, be strong and take heart and wait for the LORD" (Psalm 27:14)? When falsely accused, did he sing, "I have resolved that my mouth will not sin" (Psalm 17:3)? When afraid, did he hum,"Keep me safe, O God, for in you I take refuge" (Psalm 16:1)? Or when despairing, "Bring joy to your servant, for to you, O Lord, I lift up my soul" (Psalm 86:4)? We don't know all that happened during those waiting years, but we do know they were not wasted. God grew a great man who never lost his song or perspective. "I will exalt you, my God the King; I will praise your name for ever and ever. . . . The LORD is faithful to all his promises and loving toward all he has made" (Psalm 145:1, 13).

Question: How do I handle God's waiting times?

Faithlift: God never wastes a "wait."

MARCH 17

When [Michal] saw King David leaping and dancing before the

LORD, she despised him in her heart. 2 Samuel 6:16

Further reading: 2 Samuel 6

David and his people danced with joy; the ark of the Lord was home in Jerusalem. After offering sacrifices to God, "he blessed the people in the name of the LORD Almighty. Then he gave a loaf of bread, a cake of dates and a cake of raisins to each person in the whole crowd of Israelites, both men and women. And all the people went to their homes (vv. 18–19). Then David returned to bless his family. But Michal, wife of David and daughter of Saul, would have none of David's joy or dancing, and separate bedrooms followed. Some people can't deal with dancing or delight!

Question: Are you more of a dancer or a despiser?

Faithlift: Enjoy the dance of this day.

MARCH 18

Is there anyone still left of the house of Saul to whom I can show kindness for Jonathan's sake? 2 Samuel 9:1

Further reading: 2 Samuel 9

Powerful, popular King David didn't need entries for his "to do" list. It appeared that the people loved him and "the LORD gave David victory everywhere he went" (2 Samuel 8:14). So why should he have to go looking for someone to show kindness to, especially someone from the house of Saul, his old foe? Why? To honor his word to his friend Jonathan, Saul's son. But what good would it do Jonathan? Jonathan was dead, yes, but these friends had made an oath to their families as well. We read in 1 Samuel 20:15, "and [David], do not ever cut off your kindness from my family—not even when the LORD has cut off every one of David's enemies from the face of the earth." David remembered and reached out to locate anyone from Saul's household. The search uncovered crippled Mephibosheth, Jonathan's son. He entered David's world bowing and shivering with fear. But Mephibosheth soon learned that he had nothing to fear, for his father's friend, David, had chosen to be his friend as well.

Question: How good is your word when no one is around to check up on you?

Faithlift: God remembers his promises and reaches in friendship to you today.

MARCH 19

[Mephibosheth said to King David,] "What is your servant, that you should notice a dead dog like me?" 2 Samuel 9:8

Further reading: 2 Samuel 9

David did not respond to Mephibosheth based on his worth, but on David's word. Mephibosheth expected nothing and gained "everything that belonged to Saul and his family" (v. 9). But David went beyond what was just, beyond honoring his covenant with Jonathan, and insisted that lame Mephibosheth eat at his table "like one of the king's sons" (v. 11). David could not untangle lame Mephibosheth's feet, but he could straighten out his commitment to Jonathan. Friendship replaced fear with feasting fit for a king. Jonathan's son's gnarled feet hobbled to a place of honor at the king's table because David honored his word.

Question: Who needs the lift of eating at your table as one of your family?

Faithlift: God adopts us and invites us to His table as His sons and daughters. Imagine!

MARCH 20

In the spring, at the time when kings go off to war, David sent Joab. . . . 2 Samuel 11:1

Further reading: 2 Samuel 11

Routine, while sometimes monotonous, provides boundaries. David, king for enough years to find the springtime wars a bother, sent good old Joab. Indifferent to his duties, David became vulnerable to a more deadly war: the battle between good and evil. No man or woman, including the great king David, is strong enough to resist Satan's special forces when undressed mentally and physically for battle. We, like David, are vulnerable to sneak attacks when we drop our duties to do what feels good.

Question: What springtime duty are you sending a Joab to do for you?

Faithlift: Rejoice in the routines of this day.

MARCH 21

From the roof he saw a woman bathing . . . and David sent someone to find out about her.
2 Samuel 11:2–3

Further reading: 2 Samuel 11

David's fling began before Bathsheba. It started when he rejected his kingly duties to go off to war in springtime (v. 1). Free from the restraints of routine, David walked around his rooftop one evening and noticed a beautiful woman bathing. If he had stopped with an appreciative look, we'd never have read about it. But David, unwilling to do kingly battles, began to plot to win, at all costs, the passion at war within him. He moved swiftly from inquiring about her to acquiring her for himself. And hell's forces flashed word to headquarters: mission accomplished!

Question: Are you plotting to win a war God doesn't want you to start?

Faithlift: Relying on God's power makes hell's strategies: Missions impossible.

MARCH 22

But the thing David had done displeased the LORD. 2 Samuel 11:27

Further reading: 2 Samuel 11

No matter how swiftly David chose disobedience, the consequences came even faster. When David learned of Bathsheba's pregnancy, he moved quickly to cover his tracks. But Uriah, Bathsheba's husband and David's loyal soldier, refused to cooperate. His sense of duty contrasted starkly with David's indifference. Eventually, David ordered commander Joab to put Uriah in the midst of the battle, where he would be most vulnerable and die. David's plan worked. Uriah was killed in battle, and after the time of mourning, David sent for pregnant Bathsheba to become his wife. "[She] bore him a son. But the thing David had done displeased the LORD." Everything looked legitimate on the outside, but God saw the unseen and was not pleased.

Question: How legitimate are you on the inside?

Faithlift: God is at work today to strengthen you on the inside for the battles outside.

MARCH 23

Then Nathan said to David, "You are the man!"
2 Samuel 12:7

Further reading: 2 Samuel 12

There is a need today for Nathans—men and women of God who courageously, not maliciously, speak truth. As a divine messenger, Nathan creatively told a story that so captivated David "he burned with anger" against the man in Nathan's narrative. Then, swift as lightning and twice as electrifying, Nathan burned David with the truth: "You are the man!" Through Nathan God went on to speak to His friend, David, "I anointed you king over Israel, and I delivered you from the hand of Saul. I gave your master's house to you, and your master's wives into your arms. I gave you the house of Israel and Judah. And if all this had been too little, I would have given you even more. Why did you despise the word of the LORD by doing what is evil in his eyes?" (2 Samuel 12:7–9) What words had David despised? Basic commandments: do not murder; do not commit adultery; do not covet your neighbor's wife and, underscoring all, do not have any other gods before me. David ruled his people but not his passions. He became the villain in a twisted tale instead of God's king on the throne.

Question: What words of God's are you despising?

Faithlift: God wants to equip you to be the storyteller, not the subject matter for the story.

MARCH 24

Then David said to Nathan, "I have sinned against the LORD."
2 Samuel 12:13

Further reading: 2 Samuel 12

These six words highlight David's heart. With his back to the wall, he put his guard down, not his dukes up. When confronted by truth, David didn't cloud the issues by hedging or blaming. He confessed his sin. God forgave David but did not free him from the consequences of his sin. "The son born to you will die" (v. 14). So many casualties from an unnecessary war!

Question: When confronted, how do you respond?

Faithlift: God is ready to forgive when we are willing to confess and repent.

MARCH 25

Then David got up from the ground . . . went into the house of the LORD and worshiped.
2 Samuel 12:20

Further reading: 2 Samuel 12

David wept and pled with God to spare his son's life. He fasted and spent sleepless nights. But after learning of the death of his wee son, he got up, washed, changed his clothes, and went to worship his God. The servants were perplexed, but David wasn't. "While the child was still alive, I fasted and wept. I thought, 'Who knows? The

LORD may be gracious to me and let the child live.' But now that he is dead, why should I fast? Can I bring him back again? I will go to him, but he will not return to me" (vv. 22–23). David wasted no energy blaming God or himself. This chapter was closed, though probably never forgotten. He moved from weeping to worshiping, from finding perspective to giving comfort to Bathsheba.

Question: What do you do after you're flat on the ground?

Faithlift: Worship gives us the perspective we need to give or receive comfort.

MARCH 26

Then Amnon hated her with intense hatred. In fact, he hated her more than he had loved her.
2 Samuel 13:15

Further reading: 2 Samuel 13:1–22

The Bible paints sharp portraits which allow us to see ourselves mirrored in the painful pasts of others. David's son, Amnon, confused love with lust. That's trouble enough. But when Amnon lusted after his half-sister, Tamar, the beautiful sister of Absalom, a destructive course followed. First, he allowed his lust to consume him so that he felt sick, then he sought counsel from David's brother, Jonadab. Jonadab's advice was evil and filled with deceit. After tricking Tamar into coming to his house to care for him, Amnon ignored her pleas and forced himself on her. When finished with her, he cast her out, bolted the door, and then turned his self-hate onto the object of his lust, Tamar. The one he had loved he now hated "more than he had loved her" (v. 15).

Question: Have you tried to bolt the door on something painful in your past?

Faithlift: God, your Father, wants to help you open the door and find forgiveness and help for a new beginning.

MARCH 27

When King David heard all this, he was furious. 2 Samuel 13:21

Further reading: 2 Samuel 13

Anger has its place. David had a right to be angry when he learned that his daughter, Tamar, had been raped by her half-brother, Amnon. But anger alone is not enough. While Tamar took refuge in her brother Absalom's house, "Absalom never said a word to Amnon, either good or bad; he hated Amnon because he had disgraced his sister Tamar" (v. 22). Neither father David nor son Absolom took any action. But two years later, Absalom plotted to murder his brother Amnon. All the king's sons were invited to join Absalom and his sheepshearers near the border of Ephraim. When Amnon was "in high spirits from drinking wine" (v. 28), Absalom ordered his men to kill him. "Then all the king's sons got up, mounted their mules and fled" (v. 29). Anger has its place, but godly anger is more than rage. It focuses on discipline, just punishment, and restitution, not mere retaliation.

Question: What do you do with your anger?

Faithlift: God, your Father, is "slow to anger, abounding in love." Psalm 103:8

MARCH 28

Absalom lived two years in Jerusalem without seeing the king's face. 2 Samuel 14:28

Further reading: 2 Samuel 13:28–14:32

For three years after killing his brother Amnon, Absalom hid in Geshur. Not a day passed that David had not mourned for his son (see 2 Samuel 13:37). He longed to reach out to Absalom, but sometimes we need help to bridge the distance in strained relationships. Once again, God used a story to speak to David. Joab, David's military commander, cared for Absalom and David. So Joab sent for help from a wise woman from Tekoa and gave her a message for David. After David was caught up in the story, this woman, like Nathan the prophet, caught David with the point: "Like water spilled on the ground, which cannot be recovered, so we must die. But God does not take away life; instead, he devises ways so that a banished person may not remain estranged from him" (2 Samuel 14:14). David simply said, "Bring back the young man Absalom" (v. 21). David the king could command Absalom back to Jerusalem, but only David the father could draw an estranged son to himself. Absalom returned to Jerusalem, but for another two years he missed his father's forgiving touch. The near future would reveal the heart damage to family and nation that resulted from five faceless years between Absalom and his father, King David.

Question: How are you facing difficult relationships?

Faithlift: God loves to see you facing your problem people with His faithful love.

MARCH 29

The king and all the people with him arrived at their destination exhausted. 2 Samuel 16:14

Further reading: 2 Samuel 16

The years of estrangement from his father, David, ignited fires of rebellion in the young, handsome Absalom. Crafty and ambitious, Absalom soon "stole the hearts of the men of Israel" (see 2 Samuel 15:6). The day came when a messenger brought word to David that a conspiracy anchored in Absalom's forces hung on the horizon like black crepe. David panicked and summoned his leaders to flee Jerusalem. The entourage accompanying David included six hundred Gittites from Gath, the home of the giant Goliath. David urged them to go back and stay with "King Absalom" (v. 19), but none turned back. The people wept as they passed by, but as they approached Bahurim, "a man from the same clan as Saul's family came out from there." His name was Shimei. As David and his men moved on, Shimei walked opposite him, "cursing as he went and throwing stones at him and showering him with dirt. The king and all the people with him arrived at their destination exhausted" (vv. 13–14). David, weak and weary from unresolved conflicts and external pressures, did not need Shimei's shame heaped on him and his followers. No wonder they all arrived at their destination exhausted!

Question: Like Shimei, are you exhausting those around you with discouraging words?

Faithlift: As you travel through this day, listen to God's words of encouragement, and you will arrive refreshed.

MARCH 30

Be gentle with the young man Absalom for my sake.
2 Samuel 18:5

Further reading: 2 Samuel 18

What parental pain to have your son leading a nationwide rebellion against you! David's commanders, Joab, Abishai, and Ittai, gathered around him to accept orders and to affirm their leader. They persuaded him to remain in the city with words like "you are worth ten thousand of us" (v. 3). Of all the words David spoke to his commanders, these from his heart must have caught in his throat and reverberated in the ears of his top three men: "Be gentle with the young man Absalom for my sake" (v. 5). David knew they were loyal to him, understood their roles as the king's commanders, but the king wanted to underscore his father-heart to these three fierce warriors. He knew they had a job to do, but still he urged them, "be gentle with the young man Absalom for my sake."

Question: Who needs your gentle intervention?

Faithlift: Pass on this good news: God is gentle with you, for His sake and yours.

MARCH 31

You love those who hate you and hate those who love you.
2 Samuel 19:6

Further reading: 2 Samuel 18:29–19:8

The word that his son, Absalom, was dead slew David's heart like a sword. Shaken and sobbing, the king climbed to a room over the gateway. He wept, "O my son Absalom! My son, my son Absalom! If only I had died instead of you—O Absalom, my son, my son!" Throughout the day he mourned, and the day of victory for his troops turned into mourning as David's men "stole into the city that day as men steal in who are ashamed when they flee from battle" (v. 3). Then Joab shook David with this truth: "You love those who hate you and hate those who love you. . . . I see that you would be pleased if Absalom were alive today and all of us were dead. Now go out and encourage your men. . . ." (vv. 6–7). David listened and moved to the gateway, where he encouraged his men by his presence.

Question: Are you so preoccupied with the what ifs that you are missing the what is?

Faithlift: Give encouragement to the battle-weary around you and find joy in this day.

APRIL

APRIL 1

Never again will you go out with us to battle, so that the lamp of Israel will not be extinguished.
2 *Samuel 21:17*

Further reading: 2 Samuel 21

King David, old and battle-scarred, once again faced the Philistines. He had felled the giant Goliath years ago, but other monstrous enemies still taunted him. As the fight wore on between Israel and the Philistines, David became exhausted. When the enemy circled in for the kill, Abishai charged to his rescue. Then David's men swore to him, "Never again will you go out with us to battle, so that the lamp of Israel will not be extinguished" (v. 17). David's value was no longer in his sword but in his spirit. They needed the light of his leadership. And older, wiser David heeded their words.

Question: Are you relying on the sword—your familiar way of doing battle—when what you really need is the light of God's Spirit?

Faithlift: "This little light of mine; I'm gonna let it shine."

APRIL 2

David sang to the L*ORD the words of this song.* 2 *Samuel 22:1*

Further reading: 2 Samuel 22

David's men needed a singer more than a soldier. They wanted him safe from battle because they needed the light of his perspective. David could shine and sing because he knew his source. "You are my lamp, O LORD; the LORD turns my darkness into light" (v. 29). He sang truths of the God who rescued him, lifted him, and enabled him to "stand on the heights" (v. 34). He sang of God's faithfulness, purity, and avenging power.

Unlike Absalom and the kings before and after him, he made no monuments to himself but spoke and sang of the Lord, his rock. He exalted God, "the rock, my Savior!" (v. 47). No wonder his men wanted him out of the heat of battle. They needed a singer more than a soldier.

Question: Will you dare stand back and sing?

Faithlift: There is great power in the simple songs of faith.

April 3

David longed for water and said, "Oh, that someone would get me a drink of water from the well near the gate of Bethlehem!"
2 Samuel 23:15

Further reading: 2 Samuel 23

The battle between the Israelites and the Philistines raged on. David was safe in a cave at Adullam, but he was very thirsty. Three of his thirty mighty men, hearing him sigh for water, broke through the enemy lines and "drew water from the well near the gate of Bethlehem and carried it back to David. But he refused to drink it; instead, he poured it out before the LORD" (v. 16). How these men loved their king! And David took no advantage of that love.

Question: Would you have swallowed the water?

Faithlift: At greatest sacrifice God offers you living water; drink and live.

April 4

But the king replied to Araunah, "No, I insist on paying you for it. I will not sacrifice to the LORD my God burnt offerings that cost me nothing."
2 Samuel 24:24

Further reading: 2 Samuel 24

A plague crawled through Israel because David had sinned by counting the fighting men of Israel and Judah. David cried for mercy for his people. "'Let us fall into the hands of the LORD, for his mercy is great; but do not let me fall into the hands of men.' So the LORD sent a plague on Israel from that morning until the end of the time designated" (vv. 14–15). Seeing his people suffer, David cried out, "I am the one who has sinned and done wrong. These are but sheep. What have they done? Let your hand fall upon me and my family" (v. 17). God instructed David to build an altar on Araunah's threshing floor. When King David came to buy the threshing floor and oxen to sacrifice to the LORD, Araunah wanted to give it to him. But David insisted on paying for it. "I will not sacrifice to the Lord my God burnt offerings that cost me nothing."

Question: How much do your sacrifices cost you?

Faithlift: Follow David's example: give your best today.

April 5

His father had never interfered with him by asking, "Why do you behave as you do?" 1 Kings 1:6

Further reading: 1 Kings 1

Challenges for David's throne did not end with Absalom's death. Soon handsome Adonijah, next born after Absalom, determined to replace his father, David, as king. David had ruled the nation of Israel better then he had led his own family. Indulged, undisciplined Adonijah soon followed the path of indulged Absalom. It's better to interfere, to ask some challenging questions, and to set limits while children are growing up so we can enjoy them later as friends, not fear them as enemies.

Question: Who needs your faith-filled interference today?

Faithlift: Thank God for His holy interference.

April 6

When the time drew near for David to die, he gave a charge to Solomon his son. 1 Kings 2:1

Further reading: 1 Kings 1:28–2:12

Many years had passed since David saw beautiful Bathsheba and coveted her for himself. The son born from their affair had died, but God did not continue to punish David and Bathsheba. They had another son, Solomon, whom the Lord loved and chose to succeed David as king. What words would David reserve for his final father-son talk? David charged Solomon, "Be strong, show yourself a man, and observe what the LORD your God requires: Walk in his ways, and keep his decrees and commands, his laws and requirements, as written in the Law of Moses, so that you may prosper in all you do and wherever you go, and that the LORD may keep his promise to me: 'If your descendants watch how they live, and if they walk faithfully before me with all their heart and soul, you will never fail to have a man on the throne of Israel'" (vv. 2–4). Solomon probably knew some of the ungodly ways in which his father had demonstrated manhood, but now his father, an older and wiser King David, challenged his son to show true manhood by obeying the Lord.

Question: What are some ways our culture encourages us to show ourselves as real men or women?

Faithlift: God's strength equips you to obey and walk like real women and men.

April 7

And God said, "Ask for whatever you want me to give you."
1 Kings 3:5

Further reading: 1 Kings 3:1–15

David's challenge to his son Solomon brought immediate returns. While King David and Solomon offered sacrifices in Gibeon, the Lord spoke to Solomon one night in a dream. "Ask for whatever you want me to give you" (v. 5). What would the new king ask of God? Solomon reiterated

God's faithfulness to him as David's successor. "Now, O LORD my God, you have made your servant king in place of my father David. But I am only a little child and do not know how to carry out my duties. Your servant is here among the people you have chosen, a great people, too numerous to count or number. So give your servant a discerning heart to govern your people and to distinguish between right and wrong. For who is able to govern this great people of yours?" (vv. 7–9). Solomon, who could have asked for anything, requested wisdom! David had charged his son to "show [himself] a man" (1 Kings 2:2), and Solomon initiated his reign by doing just that! Real men and women know what they lack and seek help. Solomon was wise enough to know that he needed even more wisdom to lead God's children.

Question: How would you have answered God's question?

Faithlift: God gives you the opportunity today to ask Him for what you need most.

April 8

Moreover, I will give you what you have not asked for.
1 Kings 3:13

Further reading: 1 Kings 3:10–28

How pleased God was to hear an unselfish request! God gave Solomon what he desired. "I will give you a wise and discerning heart, so that there will never have been anyone like you, nor will there ever be" (v. 12). But God was so pleased with Solomon's wise choice that He went beyond Solomon's request. "I will give you what you have not asked for—both riches and honor—so that in your lifetime you will have no equal among kings. And if you walk in my ways and obey my statutes and commands as David your father did, I will give you a long life" (vv. 13–14). How generous is God to those who are humble and honest!

Question: Do your requests leave room for God to surprise you?

Faithlift: God loves to surprise His humble, honest children!

April 9

Then Solomon awoke—and he realized it had been a dream. 1 Kings 3:15

Further reading: 1 Kings 3:1–15

It is interesting to see how Solomon responded after he woke up and realized the scenario with God was all a dream. He didn't stretch, yawn, and splash water on his face to begin his royal day. "He returned to Jerusalem, stood before the ark of the Lord's covenant and sacrificed burnt offerings and fellowship offerings. Then he gave a feast for all his court" (v. 15). When we have heard from God—through dreams, whispers, printed word, or whatever form He selects—we must decide how we will respond to what we have heard. Will we believe and act on what we have heard? Will we question the method or messenger? Will we try a new tactic to get what we want in a way we can understand? Solomon, fully awake, chose to worship God and welcome his court by serving a feast. Fully awake leadership reaches up to God in worship and out to people in love.

Question: How awake are you?

Faithlift: A day that commences with worship and continues in works of love will never be wasted.

April 10

When all Israel heard the verdict the king had given, they held the king in awe, because they saw that he had wisdom from God to administer justice. 1 Kings 3:28

Further reading: 1 Kings 3:16–28

It must not have been long from the time Solomon asked for and received wisdom until he was called on to exercise it. Two prostitutes told him how they had given birth within three days of each other. One woman's child died, but the other's lived. One accused the other of swapping babies during the night, placing the dead child on the other mother's breast. They argued before the king as to which mother belonged with the living baby, but wise Solomon halted the dispute with his strange plan. "Bring me a sword. . . . Cut the living child in two and give half to one and half to the other" (vv. 24–25). At this horrid thought, the real mother's love for her son surfaced in sacrificial love, and she cried, "Please, my lord, give her the living baby! Don't kill him!" The other woman, however, agreed with Solomon's plan. "Neither I nor you shall have him. Cut him in two!" Then the king ruled, "Give the living baby to the first woman. Do not kill him; she is his mother" (vv. 26–27). Word of Solomon's wisdom traveled fast, and the people acknowledged the source of that wisdom: the living God.

Question: How much wisdom from God shows in your daily decisions?

Faithlift: Your decisions today can honor God.

April 11

My father David had it in his heart to build a temple for the Name of the L*ORD*, *the God of Israel. 1 Kings 8:17*

Further reading: 1 Kings 8

What a heritage—a father whose heart was filled with thoughts of God! Solomon remembered the desire of his father's heart and moved ahead with the plans to build a temple for God. God knew David's heart, but because David had been a man of war and bloodshed (see 1 Chronicles 28:3), God had chosen his son Solomon to build the temple, and Solomon had worked for years to construct it. It was magnificent! At last the day came to move the ark of the Lord into the inner sanctuary of the temple. While all the people gathered in front of the temple, Solomon turned from talking to God and turned around and blessed the people. Then the wise king prayed and dedicated the temple to God. "O LORD, God of Israel, there is no God like you in heaven above or on earth below—you who keep your covenant of love with your servants who continue wholeheartedly in your way" (v. 23). For fourteen days the people worshiped and praised God, celebrating His goodness. "On the following day [Solomon] sent the people away. They blessed the king and then went home, joyful and glad in heart for all the good the LORD had done for his servant David and his people Israel" (v. 66). David's heart for God and his desire to build a house for God extended to his son Solomon, and their joy overflowed to the people they ruled with love and wisdom.

Question: What is the next generation catching from you?

Faithlift: Heart's desires are catching!

APRIL 12

When the queen of Sheba heard about the fame of Solomon and his relation to the name of the LORD, she came to test him with hard questions. 1 Kings 10:1

Further reading: 1 Kings 10:1–13

Privatization of faith in God was not condoned in Solomon's day, nor should it be in ours. People have a need and right to know about God and our relationship to Him. The Queen of Sheba could hear the rumors for only so long. One day she determined to see and hear for herself. From what seemed like the ends of the earth she traveled with her great caravan to Jerusalem. She arrived with more than spices and gold and precious stones; the queen brought hard questions. She "talked with him about all that she had on her mind. Solomon answered all her questions; nothing was too hard for the king to explain to her" (vv. 2–3). The queen was overwhelmed, and she praised Solomon's God. She reiterated what she had heard in her own country about Solomon's wealth and wisdom and how she had longed to see and hear for herself. Then she added, "Indeed, not even half was told me; in wisdom and wealth you have far exceeded the report I heard. How happy your men must be! How happy your officials, who continually stand before you and hear your wisdom! Praise be to the LORD your God, who has delighted in you and placed you on the throne of Israel. Because of the LORD's eternal love for Israel, He has made you king, to maintain justice and righteousness" (vv. 7–9). The queen returned with more than she had brought.

Question: How do you respond to hard questions from seekers?

Faithlift: May those who seek God find your life an answer for their toughest questions.

April 13

King Solomon, however, loved many foreign women besides Pharaoh's daughter—Moabites, Ammonites, Edomites, Sidonians and Hittites. 1 Kings 11:1

Further reading: 1 Kings 10:14–11:13

The wisdom Solomon used to rule a people did not rule his passions. Once wise, King Solomon had become a foolish older man. God had clearly told the Israelites not to intermarry with foreigners who worshiped other gods. "They will surely turn your hearts after their gods" (11:2). It didn't take extra wisdom to understand such a clear command. Even the slow could grasp "Thou shalt not!" Foolish Solomon, nevertheless "held fast to them in love. He had seven hundred wives of royal birth and three hundred concubines, and his wives led him astray" (11:2–3) The God who loved Solomon was displeased with His wise king/foolish man. For "as Solomon grew old, his wives turned his heart after other gods, and his heart was not fully devoted to the LORD his God, as the heart of David his father had been" (11:4). How sad to be wise enough in youth to ask for wisdom but too foolish in old age to use it!

Question: Are you applying today wisdom you have learned from God in the past?

Faithlift: Spiritual fitness today diminishes the chance of a spiritual heart attack in old age.

APRIL 14

But Rehoboam rejected the advice the elders gave him and consulted the young men who had grown up with him and were serving him. 1 Kings 12:8

Further reading: 1 Kings 12:1–24

Solomon's choices to go after other gods brought consequences. After Solomon died, his son, Rehoboam, succeeded him as king. Rehoboam was not wise like his father. He consulted the elders who had served his father but did not follow their advice. Instead, he took the advice of his brash young peers. Their tough stance said to tell the people, "My little finger is thicker than my father's waist. My father laid on you a heavy yoke; I will make it even heavier. My father scourged you with whips; I will scourge you with scorpions" (vv. 10–11). The people rebelled at the king's harsh words, eventually crowning Jeroboam king of all but one tribe. "Only the tribe of Judah remained loyal to the house of David" (v. 20). The seed of Solomon's divided heart had taken root, bringing forth a rebellious son and a divided kingdom. When Rehoboam mustered the house of Judah and the tribe of Benjamin to fight against Israel to regain the lost kingdom, God sent word through Shemaiah, a man of God. "'Do not go up to fight against your brothers, Israelites. Go home, every one of you, for this is my doing.' So they obeyed the word of the LORD and went home again as the

LORD had ordered" (v. 24). A divided heart produced a divided kingdom.

Question: How well do you listen to your elders?

Faithlift: Go beyond asking the right questions of the right people; do what's right!

APRIL 15

You have provoked me to anger and thrust me behind your back. 1 Kings 14:9

Further reading: 1 Kings 12:25–14:20

King Jeroboam commenced his reign over the major portion of Solomon's divided kingdom in fear. Concerned that his people's loyalty would revert to the house of David when they returned to Jerusalem to worship God, Jeroboam made two golden calves and housed them in Bethel and Dan. We know that he sought advice before doing this detestable act, but the Bible does not tell us from whom. Wicked Jeroboam spoke to the people, "It is too much for you to go up to Jerusalem. Here are your gods, O Israel, who brought you up out of Egypt" (1 Kings 12:28). This king did evil in God's eyes by defying God's words and treating lightly what God held sacred, including appointing "priests for the high places from all sorts of people. Anyone who wanted to become a priest he consecrated for the high places" (1 Kings 13:33). The word of God came to Jeroboam through Ahijah the prophet, "I raised you up from among the people and made you a leader over my people Israel. I tore the kingdom away from the house of David and gave it to you, but you have not been like my servant David, who kept my commands and followed me with all his heart, doing only what was right in my eyes. You have done more evil than all who lived before you. You have made for yourself other gods, idols made of metal; you have provoked me to anger and thrust me behind your back" (vv. 7–9).

Question: What are some ways in which you thrust God behind your back?

Faithlift: To those who love the Lord it is never "too much to go up to Jerusalem" to worship God (1 Kings 12:28).

APRIL 16

He took . . . all the gold shields Solomon had made. So King Rehoboam made bronze shields to replace them. 1 Kings 14:26–27

Further reading: 1 Kings 14:21–31

The wealth, magnificence, and power of Solomon's kingdom dwindled to a divided people and land under the leadership of two wicked kings. In Rehoboam's fifth year of rule the king of Egypt attacked his small kingdom, Judah. "Shishak king of Egypt . . . carried off the treasures of the temple of the LORD and the treasures of the royal palace. He took everything, including all the gold shields Solomon had made" (vv. 25–26). How did Rehoboam respond? He made bronze shields to replace the gold ones. The palace guards picked up the bronze shields and went about their duties. Outwardly, it was business as usual; inwardly, the true treasures were gone.

Question: Have you grown content with bronzed replacements?

Faithlift: Keep seeking the true treasures of God!

APRIL 17

He did evil in the eyes of the LORD, walking in the ways of Jeroboam and in his sin, which he had caused Israel to commit. 1 Kings 15:34

Further reading: 1 Kings 15–16:8

Sin slithered through the kings of Israel like a contagious plague. One king after another chiseled the epitaph "did evil in the eyes of the Lord." When all the accomplishments were tallied, nothing mattered other than God's assessment of their reign. And nothing else matters in our kingdoms. As long as we have breath, we have time to choose again to do good in the eyes of the Lord.

Question: What words is your life chiseling for your epitaph?

Faithlift: Begin a new chapter today. Do good in God's sight.

APRIL 18

Elijah said to her, "Don't be afraid. Go home and do as you have said. But first make a small cake of bread for me."
1 Kings 17:13

Further reading: 1 Kings 17

Times were hard. Drought drained nourishment from the earth as sin had sucked life from God's children during the reign of King Ahab. God's prophet Elijah approached a widow who was gathering firewood to cook her last meal for her son and herself. To his request for food and drink she replied, "I don't have any bread—only a handful of flour in a jar and a little oil in a jug. I am gathering a few sticks to take home and make a meal for myself and my son, that we may eat it—and die" (v. 12). Elijah told her, "First make a small cake of bread for me from what you have and bring it to me, and then make something for yourself and your son. For this is what the LORD, the God of Israel, says: 'The jar of flour will not be used up and the jug of oil will not run dry until the day the LORD gives rain on the land'" (vv. 13–14). And God, as always, stayed true to His word.

Question: Would you have had the faith to feed Elijah first?

Faithlift: Trust God with your almost empty jars and jugs today.

APRIL 19

Ahab had summoned Obadiah, who was in charge of his palace. Obadiah was a devout believer in the LORD.) 1 Kings 18:3

Further reading: 1 Kings 18

Dark days characterized Ahab's reign over Israel. Ahab and his wife, Jezebel, were evil. The severe famine revealed more than physical needs. Jezebel, spiritually dried up, was hard at work killing God's prophets. But God's man Obadiah stood against her evildoing. In charge of Ahab's palace, he must have been one of the first to learn of her schemes. As a devout believer, he did what he could. "While Jezebel was killing off the LORD's prophets, Obadiah had taken a hundred prophets and hidden them in two caves, fifty in each, and had supplied them with food and water" (v. 4). What a difference one man made during the dark days of Ahab's reign!

Question: How are you using your place of influence?

Faithlift: You can dispel darkness today.

APRIL 20

When [Ahab] saw Elijah, he said to him, "Is that you, you troubler of Israel?" 1 Kings 18:16

Further reading: 1 Kings 18

Twisted Ahab called God's prophet Elijah a troublemaker! How sin warps perspective! Elijah, emboldened by God's Spirit, proclaimed, "I have not made trouble for Israel . . . but you and your father's family have. You have abandoned the LORD's commands and have followed the Baals" (v. 18). Blatantly disobedient Ahab was powerless to do anything to God's man but call him names.

Question: How much power are you giving to your namecallers?

Faithlift: Once you have been named by God, namecallers have no power over you.

APRIL 21

How long will you waver between two opinions? 1 Kings 18:21

Further reading: 1 Kings 18

Elijah, unhindered by Ahab's namecalling, told Ahab to summon the people of Israel, the 450 prophets of Baal, and four hundred prophets of Asherah to meet him on Mount Carmel. Elijah boldly challenged the people, "How long will you waver between two opinions? If the LORD is God, follow him; but if Baal is God, follow him." One would have expected the crowd with one powerful voice to shout their allegiance to God. "But the people said nothing."

Question: How would you have answered?

Faithlift: Let your *yes* to God be seen and heard today.

April 22

"O Baal, answer us!" they shouted. But there was no response; no one answered.
1 Kings 18:26

Further reading: 1 Kings 18

What a sight! Baal's frantic prophets, probably hoarse from shouting to Baal all morning long, danced around the bull on their altar. Disobedient Israel's eyeballs must have hurt from straining to see Baal's power at work. But no fire rained down from their puny god. At the time of the evening sacrifice, Elijah called the people over to him and began to rebuild the altar of the Lord, "which was in ruins" (v. 30). He then dug a trench and had four large jars of water poured on the sacrificial offering and wood. Elijah shouted, "Do it again" and "Do it a third time" and "the water ran down around the altar and even filled the trench" (vv. 34–35). Then Elijah prayed, and "the fire of the LORD fell and burned up the sacrifice, the wood, the stones and the soil, and also licked up the water in the trench. When all the people saw this, they fell prostrate and cried, 'The LORD, he is God! The LORD—he is God!'" (vv. 38–39). Baal remained silent while God rained down fire and left soil and stone sizzling.

Question: In whose God do you trust?

Faithlift: Praise the God who can ignite wet wood and hard hearts.

April 23

Elijah was afraid and ran for his life. 1 Kings 19:3

Further reading: 1 Kings 19

Is this the same man who called a showdown between hundreds of Baal's prophets and himself to demonstrate God's power and Baal's impotence? Is this the man who, having demonstrated the true God to the people of Israel, commanded the people to catch and kill all the false prophets? Yes! It is the same Elijah, courageous before thousands of God's disobedient children but now cowering under the threat of one evil woman, Jezebel. She sent word that she was going to get him "by this time tomorrow" (v. 2). And, weary from the showdown, Elijah believed Jezebel more than Jehovah.

Question: How vulnerable are you to the wrong voices when you are weary?

Faithlift: God's view of us is not limited by our view of Him.

April 24

Take my life; I am no better than my ancestors. 1 Kings 19:4

Further reading: 1 Kings 19

Weary in body and spirit, Elijah collapsed under a broom tree and prayed that he might die. "I have had enough, LORD. . . . Take my life; I am no better than my ancestors" (v. 4). How did God respond to such despair in one of his greatest men? Did God blast him for suicidal thoughts? No, God sent an angel to touch, feed, and revive him. Exhausted and filled with fear, Elijah compared himself to others and despaired. But God, filled with grace and compassion, winged a care package to His pooped prophet.

Question: How do you expect God to respond to you when you are discouraged and depressed?

Faithlift: Look for a care package from God.

April 25

What are you doing here, Elijah?
1 Kings 19:9

Further reading: 1 Kings 19

Refreshed by an angel from God, Elijah traveled forty days and nights until he reached Horeb, "the mountain of God. There he went into a cave and spent the night" (vv. 8–9). There comes a time when we, like Elijah, have to stop running and answer God's query. Elijah poured out his assessment of the Israelites, his fears, and his loneliness (see v. 10). Then God taught His tethered servant through winds, earthquakes, and fires. After the fire came a gentle whisper. . . . and it was God. When Elijah heard that voice, "he pulled his cloak over his face and went out and stood at the mouth of the cave" (v. 13). God draws us out of hiding and dares us to venture forth again.

Question: Where is your cave?

Faithlift: Listen for God's whispers of encouragement today, then venture out again.

April 26

I am the only one left, and now they are trying to kill me too.
1 Kings 19:14

Further reading: 1 Kings 19:1–14

Have you ever felt this way? Elijah, alone and discouraged, spoke from his heart to God. "I have been very zealous for the LORD God Almighty. The Israelites have rejected your covenant, broken down your altars, and put your prophets to death with the sword. I am the only one left, and now they are trying to kill me, too" (v. 14). How did God respond to Elijah? God directed him to his next assignment and declared to Elijah how many were still really with him. "I reserve seven thousand in Israel—all whose knees have not bowed down to Baal and all whose mouths have not kissed him" (v. 18). God did not rebuke Elijah; He reminded Elijah of His purpose and revealed a people untouched by idolatry. Fresh revelations from God moved Elijah from his cave to complete God's mission.

Question: What do you do when you feel you're the only one left?

Faithlift: Listen for God's declarations and directions to you today; you're not alone.

April 27

There is still one man through whom we can inquire of the LORD, but I hate him.
1 Kings 22:8

Further reading: 1 Kings 22

Ahab, king of Israel, and Jehoshaphat, king of Judah, were striking an agreement to join forces in their effort to regain Ramoth Gilead. But before the pen hit the parchment, Jehoshaphat said to Ahab, "First seek the counsel of the LORD." So Ahab sent for his prophets, about four hundred of them. Of course, they concurred and urged this evil alliance. "'Go,' they answered, 'for the LORD will give it into the king's hand'" (v. 6). But Jehoshaphat, probably uneasy with these pitiful prophets, asked, "Is there not a prophet of the LORD here whom we can inquire of?" (v. 7). Ahab's eyes must have reddened at the thought of God's man, Micaiah. Then King Ahab confessed, "There is still one man through whom we can inquire of the LORD, but I hate him because he never prophesies anything good about me, but always bad. He is Micaiah son of Imlah" (v. 8). And King Jehoshaphat said, "The king [Ahab] should not say that" (v. 8). Men and women like Micaiah who speak God's truth have never been popular; neither are the

Jehoshaphats who challenge the insights of the Ahabs. We need more who speak God's truth and fewer who live to hear only good words.

Question: How uneasy are you with man's good words?

Faithlift: Be that man or woman on whom others can count to speak God's truth.

April 28

But someone drew his bow at random and hit the king of Israel between the sections of his armor. 1 Kings 22:34

Further reading: 1 Kings 22:1–40

Ahab hated Micaiah, God's prophet, "because he never prophesie[d] anything good about [him]" (v. 8). Ahab, like most of us, put the blame on others. But Micaiah was loyal to God and spoke His truth. The consequences were a slap in the face from a false prophet and a prison sentence with bread and water until Ahab returned safely from battle. Micaiah knew he was in for a long haul because God had spoken through him. "If you ever return safely, the LORD has not spoken through me. Then he added, "Mark my words, all you people!" (v. 28). Brash, evil Ahab disguised himself and went to battle. Though the king of Aram ordered his chariot commanders not to waste their shots on anyone but King Ahab, "someone drew his bow at random and hit the king of Israel between the sections of his armor" and Ahab died a slow death (see vv. 34–38). The best disguise did not hide him or his sins from God.

Question: Which man was really in prison?

Faithlift: A diet of bread and water with God is better than a feast with lesser gods.

April 29

Let me inherit a double portion of your spirit. 2 Kings 2:9

Further reading: 2 Kings 2

Powerful Elijah was about to leave this world. His understudy, Elisha, must have been shaken at the thought of losing his mentor. At the Jordan's edge he watched Elijah pull up his cloak, strike the water, and watch it roll up, and hug the edges of the riverbank while they walked through on dry land (see v. 8). Once on the other side, Elijah asked what he could do for Elisha before he left for good. Elisha's heart answered swiftly, Give me a "double portion of your spirit" (v. 9). And "Elijah went up to heaven in a whirlwind" (v. 11), leaving behind his cloak. Then Elisha took the cloak, and struck the water of the Jordan, and it divided and he crossed over. And the company of prophets watching from the sidelines said, "The spirit of Elijah is resting on Elisha" (v. 15). Elisha had received his wish.

Question: What are you wishing for from God?

Faithlift: People on the sidelines are looking to see God's Spirit in you; keep Him visible in your marketplace.

April 30

Don't ask for just a few.
2 Kings 4:3

Further reading: 2 Kings 4:1–7

The widow of a man from the school of prophets stood bent and wrapped in the darkness of despair. Her earthly goods had gone to the creditors, and now she waited for them to come and take her two sons as slaves. When Elisha the prophet heard her wails, he asked her what she had in her house. "Just a little oil," she replied (see v. 2). Elisha told her to gather empty jars from her neighbors, emphasizing, "Don't ask for just a few" (v. 3). She and her sons began to pour the little bit of oil into the first jar, as Elisha had commanded. As the widow poured, her sons brought the next empty container. This continued until she ran out of jars. They were in the oil business! Then God's man Elisha, said, "Go, sell the oil and pay your debts. You and your sons can live on what is left" (v. 7). What a God!

Question: What if the widow had been afraid to think big?

Faithlift: Think big and start gathering jars for God's oil business.

MAY

MAY 1

Let's make a small room on the roof and put in it a bed and a table, a chair and a lamp for him. 2 *Kings 4:10*

Further reading: 2 Kings 4:8–37

Some people have the gift of hospitality. This well-to-do woman from Shunem was one of them. She used her means to bless and refresh others. She had discerned that Elisha was God's prophet, but she also knew that he was hungry and tired. She and her husband anticipated his needs for rest, reflection, and reading. They gave the best they had, and God rewarded them by giving this childless couple a son. God rewarded her hospitality to His prophet with the desire of her heart.

Question: When was the last time you were refreshed by the hospitality of one of God's thoughtful children?

Faithlift: Refresh someone soon with a body and soul stopover at your expense and for God's pleasure.

MAY 2

"Everything is all right," she said. 2 *Kings 4:26*

Further reading: 2 Kings 4:8–37

The hospitable woman from Shunem gave birth to a son about a year later, just as Elisha had prophesied. "The child grew, and one day he went out to his father, who was with the reapers" (v. 18). Out in the fields he fell sick, and they rushed him home to his mother, where he later died on her lap (see v. 20). How did she react? She put the child on the prophet's bed, saddled a donkey, and took off to find the prophet Elisha on Mount Carmel. When

Gehazi, Elisha's servant, saw her coming, he asked, "Are you all right? Is your husband all right? Is your child all right?" And she responded, "Everything is all right" (v. 26). Faith talks that way. Faith also knows who can handle the tough assignments.

Question: How would you have answered?

Faithlift: Faith neither denies the facts nor limits God.

MAY 3

Why does this fellow send someone to me to be cured of his leprosy? 2 Kings 5:7

Further reading: 2 Kings 5

Naaman was a great soldier and commander in King Aram's army. He was "a great man in the sight of his master and highly regarded . . . but he had leprosy" (v. 1). When Naaman requested the king's permission to travel to Samaria to meet with the prophet Elisha, the king gave his blessing and sent a letter to the king of Israel. "With this letter I am sending my servant Naaman to you so that you may cure him of his leprosy" (v. 6). A pagan king and his commander reached out with humble faith and desperate need to the king of Israel and the God he served. But the king of Israel suffered from a disease greater than leprosy; an uncharitable heart and suspicious nature sapped life from him, leaving him with a salty tongue. "As soon as the king of Israel read the letter, he tore his robes and said, 'Am I God? Can I kill and bring back life? Why does this fellow send someone to me to be cured of his leprosy? See how he is trying to pick a quarrel with me!'" (v. 7) Instead of reaching out in love and compassion to Naaman and leading him to the God who heals sins and lesser diseases, he ripped his robes and refused to help.

Question: Do you see yourself more often as the letter writer or the robe ripper?

Faithlift: Be like your Master, write, reach out; leave the ripping and refusing to those who serve lesser gods.

MAY 4

Now bands from Aram had gone out and had taken captive a young girl from Israel, and she served Naaman's wife.
2 Kings 5:2

Further reading: 2 Kings 5

How terrifying for the parents of this young girl! Perhaps she had been playing with a couple of friends when the men on horses plucked her up and whisked her away to live among strange people who worshiped stranger gods. How her parents must have longed for their daughter and wondered what good could come from such a cruel act. But God was at work through this young girl. She influenced Naaman's wife to persuade her leprous husband to seek healing from Elisha, the prophet, in Israel. As a result, Naaman traveled to Israel, obeyed Elisha's counsel to dip in the Jordan seven times, and returned home proclaiming, "Now I know that there is no God in all the world except in Israel" (v. 15.)

Question: What would a foreign culture learn from you about your God?

Faithlift: Serve so well that your master will listen when you share your faith.

MAY 5

My father, if the prophet had told you to do some great thing, would you not have done it?
2 Kings 5:13

Further reading: 2 Kings 5

Even though Naaman knew little or nothing of the God of Israel, common sense told him that dipping in the Jordan River seven times was an unlikely way to be cured of leprosy or anything else of consequence! The prophet Elisha stumped and angered this military man with such illogical and unheroic methodology. "Naaman went away angry and said, 'I thought that he would surely come out to me and stand and call on the name of the LORD his God, wave his hand over the spot and cure me of my leprosy'" (v. 11). But Naaman's servants prevailed. "My father, if the prophet had told you to do some great thing, would you not have done it?" (v. 13) So mighty Naaman inched toward the river with childlike faith, dipped seven times, and came up "clean like that of a young boy" (v. 14). No big deal for one great God!

Question: How do you respond to God's simple instructions?

Faithlift: God rewards those who refuse to be too big to respond in childlike faith.

May 6

As surely as the LORD lives, whom I serve, I will not accept a thing. 2 Kings 5:16

Further reading: 2 Kings 5

Naaman stood before the prophet Elisha. Such a short while ago, minus seven dips in the Jordan River, leprosy had clung to Naaman like barnacles on a boat's hull. Now he surveyed spotless skin and longed to give tangible thanks to Elisha for being God's healing hand. Elisha probably had many needs. As a prophet, Elisha would not have drawn a big salary or attractive fringe benefits. He would have experienced more pain than gain. Elisha was no masochist, but he knew his master was the God of heaven and earth, and that was sufficient reward. He could not accept a gift for that which God had given through him to Naaman. Such integrity!

Question: How would you have responded to Naaman's understandable generosity?

Faithlift: Who you serve determines what you are content to receive.

May 7

My master was too easy on Naaman. 2 Kings 5:20

Further reading: 2 Kings 5

Gehazi, Elisha's servant, watched Naaman's caravan head back to Aram with the unclaimed goodies. He had heard his master refuse gifts for good deeds and must have questioned his sanity. Perhaps he mused, "God or Elisha may not need pay, but I could use a little extra. Besides, Naaman will feel better if this healing costs him something. Most of us don't trust something for nothing. We like to earn our way." Gehazi ran after the caravan, concocting a story about two needy young men from the company of prophets and receiving from Naaman two talents (about 150 pounds) of silver and two sets of clothing. Once home, he hid the goods before he headed for Elisha. The wise prophet probed his wicked servant about his whereabouts; and Gehazi, adept at lying, answered, "Your servant didn't go anywhere" (v. 25). Then God, who had healed Naaman, hit greedy Gehazi with a leprosy so fierce that it clung to his descendants forever (see v. 27).

Question: Are you endangering the next generation by your greed?

Faithlift: Be wise about what you run after; you may catch more than you've bargained for.

May 8

"Don't be afraid," the prophet answered. "Those who are with us are more than those who are with them." 2 Kings 6:16

Further reading: 2 Kings 6

Elisha's servant was understandably shaken. Awakening early, he had found the city of Dothan surrounded by an enemy army with many horses and chariots. As Elisha's servant, he must have seen more than one miracle and experienced more than one major obstacle. But this was more than major; this looked impossible! The panicked servant ran to Elisha, who prayed, "O LORD, open his eyes so he may see" (v. 17). And God let one timid man see the tremendous hosts of heaven who surrounded the enemy. No wonder Elisha could say, "Don't be afraid . . . those who are with us are more than those who are with them" (v. 16). And so it is today!

Question: How well do your eyes of faith see?

Faithlift: Look up and see; God has your enemy surrounded!

MAY 9

Then they said to each other, "We're not doing right. This is a day of good news and we are keeping it to ourselves."
2 Kings 7:9

Further reading: 2 Kings 7

The Arameans kept a stranglehold on Samaria through fear and famine. The people's hunger was so great that they were devouring donkey heads and doves' dung. While the king of Israel blamed the prophet Elisha for their ills, four lepers decided they had nothing to lose by leaving town and surrendering to the enemy. But when they arrived at the Arameans' camp, no one met them. "For the Lord had caused the Arameans to hear the sound of chariots and horses and a great army. . . . They left the camp as it was and ran for their lives" (vv. 6–7). The four outcasts ate, drank, looted, and hid their plunder, then repeated the process. Suddenly conscience-stricken, they declared, "We're not doing right. This is a day of good news and we are keeping it to ourselves" (v. 9). And God allowed four social rejects to be His special relayers of good news.

Question: Is there good news that you are hoarding?

Faithlift: Relay God's good news to the hungry world around you.

MAY 10

They followed worthless idols and themselves became worthless.
2 Kings 17:15

Further reading: 2 Kings 17:1–23

The Old Testament comments on many kings who "did evil in the eyes of the Lord." Hoshea was no exception. He was seized and imprisoned by the Assyrians, and the nation he had ruled was exiled to Assyria. God used pagan leaders to punish His disobedient children. God had repeatedly warned the Israelites not to worship other gods, "but they would not listen and were as stiff-necked as their fathers, who did not trust in the LORD their God" (v. 14). Eventually, they became as worthless as the worthless idols they followed. They forsook God, worshiped idols they had fashioned with their own hands, sacrificed their sons and daughters to these gods that would never be satisfied, and practiced sorcery and divination (see vv. 16–17). What a waste of people and their divine purpose!

Question: Would you like to become like the God of Israel or like other gods you may follow?

Faithlift: The world needs to see more children who clearly resemble their Father God.

MAY 11

Hezekiah trusted in the LORD, the God of Israel. 2 Kings 18:5

Further reading: 2 Kings 18:1–8

Such a simple statement hardly seems worth singling out of the Old Testament. Yet, after reading about king after king who "did evil in the sight of the Lord," citing one who trusted in the Lord seems highly noteworthy. God must have been impressed, too, for "the LORD was with him; he was successful in whatever he undertook" (v. 7). Hezekiah demonstrated his trust in visible ways before his people. "He removed the high places, smashed the sacred stones and . . . broke into pieces the bronze snake Moses had made, for up to that time the Israelites had been burning incense to it" (v. 4). Hezekiah turned his people from worthless gods to worship the true God. Such a simple statement: He "trusted in the LORD." Such a significant way to live and lead!

Question: What is noteworthy about your life today?

Faithlift: Live a noteworthy day through your trust and obedience.

MAY 12

On what are you basing this confidence of yours? 2 Kings 18:19

Further reading: 2 Kings 18:9–37

King Hezekiah's back was to the wall, and the Assyrian king taunted him and his people. When a few of Hezekiah's men heard the Assyrian king's messengers, they begged them to speak in Aramaic instead of in Hebrew so the Israelites would not be able to understand. But the Assyrian commander belted out, "Do not let Hezekiah persuade you to trust in the LORD when he says, 'The LORD will surely deliver us; this city will not be given into the hand of the king of Assyria'" (v. 30). What tough times for timid folks! How the children of Israel, from King Hezekiah to kids within earshot, must have shivered! In their own power the nation of Judah was in a no-win situation, surrounded by the powerful Assyrians. The enemy's taunts usually drown out the petitions of God's children. But God's power is greater than the strongest enemy army!

Question: On what are you basing your confidence today?

Faithlift: Your simple trust in God is more than a match for the enemy's taunts!

MAY 13

Choose life and not death! 2 Kings 18:32

Further reading: 2 Kings 18:9–37

This verse sounds like Moses' words to the children of Israel. "I have set before you life and death, blessings and curses. Now choose life, so that you and your children may live and that you may love the LORD your God, listen to his voice and hold fast to him. For the LORD is your life . . . " (Deuteronomy 30:19–20). But the speaker in 2 Kings is an enemy of God's children. The king of Assyria had sent these words to entice the Israelites to forsake the God of their fathers and follow after lesser gods: "Make peace with me and come out to me. Then every one of you will eat from his own vine and fig tree and drink water from his own cistern, until I come and take you to a land like your own, a land of grain and new wine, a land of bread and vineyards, a land of olives trees and honey. Choose life and not death!" (vv. 31–32). How tempting it is to listen to the wrong voice!

Question: What offer of life are you accepting today?

Faithlift: Listen to God and live!

MAY 14

But the people remained silent and said nothing in reply, because the king had commanded, "Do not answer him."
2 Kings 18:36

Further reading: 2 Kings 18:9–37

Have you ever been ensnared in a futile argument? Then you know why King Hezekiah commanded his people to remain silent before the taunts of the Assyrians. There was no way, in human terms, that the children of Israel could win a word battle! To every tormenting question they would have had to answer no. Had the god of any nation ever delivered his land from the hand of the king of Assyria? No. Had they rescued Samaria from the Assyrian king's hand? No. How then could the Lord deliver Jerusalem from the Assyrian king's hand? (see vv. 33–35) What self-control to remain silent when squeezed!

Question: How does your tongue respond to taunts?

Faithlift: What you don't say today may be your best sermon.

MAY 15

When King Hezekiah's officials came to Isaiah, Isaiah said to them, "Tell your master, 'This is what the LORD says: Do not be afraid of what you have heard—those words with which the underlings of the king of Assyria have blasphemed me.'"
2 Kings 19:5–6

Further reading: 2 Kings 19

When King Hezekiah heard from some of his royal staff what was being said about him and his God, he tore his royal robes, put on sackcloth, headed for the temple, and sent two of his staff to the prophet Isaiah. Under great stress, Hezekiah made all the right moves. And Isaiah sent encouragement to God's mourning monarch. He let Hezekiah know that God had heard and that Hezekiah should not fear the Assyrian king's words. God, not the children of Israel, was their real target. Now those were words to trust!

Question: Whose words are you trusting?

Faithlift: Under stress, head for God and hear His words of encouragement.

MAY 16

It is true, O LORD, that the Assyrian kings have laid waste these nations and their lands. They have thrown their gods into the fire and destroyed them, for they were not gods but only wood and stone, fashioned by men's hands. 2 Kings 19:17–18

Further reading: 2 Kings 19

King Hezekiah, his head full of threats from the king of Assyria, went to the temple and spread the letter out before the Lord, whom the Assyrians were blaspheming. Hezekiah didn't behave like a man full of fear or panic; he behaved like a realist. "It is true, O LORD, that the Asyrian kings have laid waste these nations and their lands" (v. 17). In other words, their future didn't look good if God didn't intervene. Hezekiah recognized that the other nations had lesser gods of wood and stone which the Assyrians could easily destroy. But Hezekiah did more than recognize the facts; he relayed his faith. "Now, O LORD our God, deliver us from his hand, so that all kingdoms on earth may know that you alone, O LORD, are God (v. 19). And God did just that!

Question: Where would you head with such threatening news?

Faithlift: Do more than recognize the facts; relay your faith!

MAY 17

Then Isaiah son of Amoz sent a message to Hezekiah: "This is what the LORD, the God of Israel, says: I have heard your prayer concerning Sennacherib king of Assyria." 2 Kings 19:20

Further reading: 2 Kings 19

The watching, listening God knew Hezekiah's heart and heard him plead with the people to keep their trust in God. His anger burned against the Assyrians, and He yearned to save the children He loved. "I will defend this city and save it, for my sake and for the sake of David my servant," declared the LORD (v. 34). And that night "the angel of the Lord went out and put to death one hundred and eighty-five thousand men in the Assyrian camp. When the people got up the next morning—there were all the dead bodies! So Sennacherib king of Assyria broke camp and withdrew. He returned to Nineveh and stayed there. One day, while he was worshiping in the temple of his god Nisroch, his sons Adrammelech and Sharezer cut him down with the sword, and they escaped to the land of Ararat. And Esarhaddon his son succeeded him as king" (vv. 35–37). God heard Hezekiah's prayer and took action. The Assyrians met a God like no other but never lived to tell it.

Question: How do you know this great God?

Faithlift: As you see God at work today, live to tell it.

MAY 18

In those days Hezekiah became ill and was at the point of death. The prophet Isaiah son of Amoz went to him and said, "This is what the LORD says: Put your house in order, because you will die; you will not recover."
2 Kings 20:1

Further reading: 2 Kings 20:1–11

Hezekiah heard the grim report and responded as he had in previous seemingly no-win situations. He "turned his face to the wall and prayed to the LORD" (v. 2). He had prayed when he learned that the Assyrians planned to capture him and Jerusalem. He prayed now, when he learned that his life was almost over. He cried, "'Remember, O LORD, how I have walked before you faithfully and with wholehearted devotion and have done what is good in your eyes.' And Hezekiah wept bitterly" (v. 3). The God who had heard Hezekiah urge his people to trust God with their lives now heard him cry for his own life. Then Isaiah, who had brought such bad tidings, delivered the good news. "I have heard your prayer and seen your tears; I will heal you . . . I will add fifteen years to your life" (v. 5–6). There is no God like this God.

Question: What would you need to do if God told you today to put your house in order?

Faithlift: God remembers when you have walked faithfully. Keep on!

MAY 19

[The son of the] king of Babylon sent Hezekiah letters and a gift, because he had heard of Hezekiah's illness. Hezekiah received the messengers and

showed them all that was in his storehouses. 2 Kings 20:12–13

Further reading: 2 Kings 20:12–21

This was no small miracle. King Hezekiah, near death, had now received fifteen more years of life from God. The word traveled even to pagan potentates like the king of Babylon. They must have been curious about the God of Hezekiah, who had wiped out the Assyrians without chariots, armies, or horse. And now He had taken a personal interest in Hezekiah and extended his life. What news! But Hezekiah chose to focus, not on God's power, but on his possessions. The Babylonians wanted to learn of spiritual treasures, but Hezekiah showed them only his storehouse trinkets.

Question: What are you showing those who long to learn of the treasure within you?

Faithlift: Show your world the treasures, not the trinkets.

MAY 20

Manasseh [son of Hezekiah] was twelve years old when he became king . . . he did evil in the eyes of the LORD, following the detestable practices of the nations the LORD had driven out before the Israelites. 2 Kings 21:1–2

Further reading: 2 Kings 21

Manasseh was born to Hezekiah during the fifteen-year extension granted by God. How did Hezekiah live during those years? How could the people say of Hezekiah, "There was no one like him among all the kings of Judah, either before him or after him. He held fast to the LORD and did not cease to follow Him; he kept the commands the LORD had given Moses" (2 Kings 18:5–6), and yet describe his son Manasseh as one who "did evil in the eyes of the LORD. . . . He rebuilt the high places his father Hezekiah had destroyed; he also erected altars to Baal. . . . He bowed down to all the starry hosts and worshiped them. He built altars. . . . He sacrificed his own son in the fire, practiced sorcery and divination, and consulted mediums and spiritists" (vv. 2–6). How tragic that historians could not write, "like father, like son."

Question: In what ways are you strengthening the faith of the next generation?

Faithlift: May those who take note of you today see a strong resemblance between you and your Father God.

MAY 21

Josiah was eight years old when he became king, and he reigned in Jerusalem thirty-one years. . . . He did what was right in the eyes of the LORD and walked in all the ways of his father David, not turning aside to the right or to the left. 2 Kings 22:1–2

Further reading: 2 Kings 22

Josiah was the grandson of Manasseh, a wicked king, and the son of Amon, a king who "did evil in the eyes of the LORD, as his father Manasseh had done" (2 Kings 21:20). Yet, when Josiah became king at the age of eight, he began doing "what was right in the eyes of the LORD." What an encouraging example for any who have allowed their pasts to limit their future! God, your Father, is greater than any family liabilities you may have inherited. It is possible to be a Josiah and to do what is right in God's eyes, no matter how old you are or how evil your family history.

Question: Which family are you allowing to influence your present and future?

Faithlift: Be a Josiah and begin a fresh chapter on your family history.

MAY 22

They were brave warriors, famous men, and heads of their families. But they were unfaithful to the God of their fathers and prostituted themselves to the gods of the peoples of the land, whom God had destroyed before them. 1 Chronicles 5:24–25

Further reading: 1 Chronicles 5

Most of us would be content to be included on any one of those lists: brave warriors, famous men, or heads of families! But God was not satisfied with people who were merely brave, famous, or heads of families. All knowing, always faithful, God expects His children to be faithful. What good is a brave warrior in the wrong army? Of what value is fame if you're revered for insignificant choices? How stable is your headship if you yourself are under no worthy authority? No wonder God is not impressed with the brave, famous, and heads of families who are unfaithful to Him.

Question: What would you like written of you?

Faithlift: There's no higher honor than to make God's faithful list.

MAY 23

All these were descendants of Asher—heads of families, choice men, brave warriors and outstanding leaders. 1 Chronicles 7:40

Further reading: 1 Chronicles 7:30–40

It is interesting to note that heads of families leads this list of distinctive qualities in Asher's descendants. The order in the list may not have great significance. But there is long-term impact on families and on a culture where family focus and leadership in the home is second to being choice, brave, or outstanding in the community. It's worth some thought.

Question: Where is your focus?

Faithlift: God will help you focus on His priorities.

MAY 24

Day after day men came to help David, until he had a great and mighty army. 1 Chronicles 12:22

Further reading: 1 Chronicles 12:1–22

Jealous, fearful King Saul banished innocent David from his

presence and forced him to live like an outlaw. But word spread quickly that God's hand rested upon David, and great and mighty men defected to David's side. "They came to Hebron fully determined to make David king over all Israel. All the rest of the Israelites were also of one mind to make David king" (v. 38). People around us know when there is something different about us. God's mark on our lives draws others to Him, and His army grows daily. Our one intent is to make Him king.

Question: When others watch your life, to which side are they attracted?

Faithlift: God's best recruiter is a joyful, faithful soldier.

May 25

Then all the people left, each for his own home, and David returned home to bless his family.
1 Chronicles 16:43

Further reading: 1 Chronicles 16

This had been an extraordinary time of celebration for King David and his people. The ark of God was back in Jerusalem. The ark contained "the two stone tablets that Moses had placed in it at Horeb, where the LORD made a covenant with the Israelites after they came out of Egypt" (1 Kings 8:9). King David was the life of the party as they danced, sang, ate, and praised God through songs, offerings, prayers, and thanks. King David led them in a song of praise he had written for God. No wonder, when it was all over, "David returned home to bless his family."

Question: What difference does it make to your family when you return home?

Faithlift: Your relationship with God spills over to bless those closest to you.

May 26

Now then, tell my servant David, "This is what the LORD Almighty says: I took you from the pasture and from following the flock, to be ruler over my people Israel." 1 Chronicles 17:7

Further reading: 1 Chronicles 17:1–15

What an amazing God! Who else would head for a pasture to select a king? Who else would choose one who tended a flock of sheep to tend the flock of Israel? Who else would take a young shepherd's staff and exchange it for a royal scepter? Only our God!

Question: Can you believe God sees you in your pasture and has some royal plans for your life?

Faithlift: God has a royal reward for those who lovingly, faithfully tend the flock at hand until He moves them to another pasture or palace—a matter of perspective.

May 27

Then King David went in and sat before the LORD, and he said: "Who am I, O LORD God, and what is my family, that you have brought me this far?" 1 Chronicles 17:16

Further reading: 1 Chronicles 17:16–27

God's prophet Nathan reported to David all that God had told him. David's ears hummed with sweet, strong promises from his Father God. "I will be his father, and he will be my son. I will never take my love away from him, as I took it away from your predecessor. I will set him over my house and my kingdom forever; his throne will be established forever" (vv. 13–14). How did David respond to such security and affirmation? He sat humbly before the Lord and spoke from his heart: "Who am I, O LORD God, and what is my family, that you have brought me this far?" The answer lies not in who we are but in who God is. "There is no one like you, O LORD" (v. 20).

Question: "Who am I, O LORD God, and what is my family, that you have brought me this far?"

Faithlift: Praise the Lord God who has brought you this far.

MAY 28

David said, "My son Solomon is young and inexperienced, and the house to be built for the LORD should be of great magnificence and fame and splendor in the sight of all the nations. Therefore I will make preparations for it." So David made extensive preparations before his death.
1 Chronicles 22:5

Further reading: 1 Chronicles 22

How David wanted to build a house for the Lord! But God said no to David and yes to David's son. David didn't pout, however. Instead, he made preparations which would ensure Solomon's success and a magnificent house for his God. Neither self-centeredness nor sluggishness characterized David's last years. Rather, he came alongside his son and gave him the treasures of a lifetime: wealth and wisdom. The wise father reminded his son of God's presence, purpose, and promises. What a sight for a watching world—David, perhaps with his arm around Solomon's shoulders, exhorting and encouraging his son. "Be strong and courageous. Do not be afraid or discouraged" (v. 13). What a significant way for a dad to leave this world—by launching a godly son!

Question: What preparations are you making to encourage and support those who will follow you?

Faithlift: Make preparations today for someone else's success.

MAY 29

And you, my son Solomon, acknowledge the God of your father, and serve him with wholehearted devotion and with a willing mind, for the LORD searches every heart and understands every motive behind the thoughts. If you seek him, he will be found by you; but if you forsake him, he will reject you forever. 1 Chronicles 28:9

Further reading: 1 Chronicles 28:1–10

David chose to give Solomon a father/son talk in front of all Israel. He charged his son to "be careful to follow all the commands of the LORD your God, that you may possess this good land and pass it on as an inheritance to your descendants forever" (v. 8). King David went on to remind Solomon to serve and seek God with his whole heart. Listening Israelites were reminded with Solomon that their God did not play tricks on them. "If you seek him, he will be found by you." That's good news for Solomon and the rest of us seekers.

Question: Are you playing hide or seek with God?

Faithlift: God is waiting to be found by you today.

MAY 30

David also said to Solomon his son, "Be strong and courageous, and do the work. Do not be afraid or discouraged, for the LORD God, my God, is with you. He will not fail you or forsake you until all the work for the service of the temple of the LORD is finished." 1 Chronicles 28:20

Further reading: 1 Chronicles 28:11–21

There comes a time to do the work. David's work was finished; it was time for Solomon's to begin. There's just so much any good parent can do. The words of wisdom and wealth passed from father to son must have energized Solomon for the enormous task ahead. But nothing matched "the LORD God, *my God,* is with you." Solomon knew that his father was old and would die before the temple was complete. David knew that Solomon could not complete it alone. So he gave his son the best he had: "*My* God, is with you." What an inheritance!

Question: What is the best you have to pass on?

Faithlift: That same God is with you today.

MAY 31

With all my resources I have provided for the temple of my God . . . besides, in my devotion to the temple of my God I now give my personal treasures of gold and silver for the temple of my God, over and above everything I have provided for this holy temple.
1 Chronicles 29:2–3

Further reading: 1 Chronicles 29:1–9

King David poured his resources—wealth, wisdom, relationships, and experience—into building God's house. Then love overtook zealous planning and giving, and David dug into his personal treasuries. Nothing was too good for his God! Gold and silver spilled out to overlay the walls of the temple. Having led by example, King David turned to his people and asked, "Now, who is willing to consecrate himself today to the LORD?" (v. 5) David could ask the question because he had answered with his life.

Question: How have your personal treasures been affected by your love for God?

Faithlift: Your best personal treasure is *you!*

JUNE

JUNE 1

But who am I, and who are my people, that we should be able to give as generously as this? Everything comes from you, and we have given you only what comes from your hand.
1 Chronicles 29:14

Further reading: 1 Chronicles 29:1–20

The story of David's silver and gold pouring into the temple's building fund finds its genesis in David's affections, not in his accountant. He didn't check to see what he needed to donate to gain a tax advantage or some good press with his people. David's generosity found its impetus, not in excessive resources, but in an enduring relationship with his God. His heart controlled his purse; not the other way around.

Question: What is the source of your generosity?

Faithlift: Look for ways to be generous with what God has given you.

JUNE 2

Hiram king of Tyre replied by letter to Solomon: "Because the LORD *loves his people, he has made you their king."*
2 Chronicles 2:11

Further reading: 2 Chronicles 2:1–18

Young King Solomon, faced with the awesome task of ruling God's children, asked God for wisdom. God granted his request and added wealth and honor. After his father, King David, died, Solomon gave orders to build the temple for the Lord God. He wrote to the king of Tyre and asked for cedar logs and skilled workers in gold, silver, bronze, iron, purple, crimson, blue yarn, engraving, and wood cutting. The letter contained more than requests; it underscored his relationship with God. "The temple I am going to build will be great, because our God is greater than all other gods" (v. 5). No doubt word of Solomon's might and wealth reached King Hiram long before Solomon's letter. Somehow, hearing about Solomon and receiving a letter from him made King Hiram exclaim, "Because the LORD loves his people, he has made you their king." That's some endorsement!

Question: Who has God placed you in contact with, because of His great love?

Faithlift: Thank God for someone He sent to demonstrate His love to you.

JUNE 3

The trumpeters and singers joined in unison, as with one voice, to give praise and thanks to the LORD. Accompanied by trumpets, cymbals and other instruments, they raised their voices in praise to the LORD and sang: "He is good; his love endures forever." Then the temple of the LORD was filled with a cloud, and the priests could not perform their service because of the cloud, for the glory of the LORD filled the temple of God.
2 Chronicles 5:13–14

Further reading: 2 Chronicles 5

What a day of extraordinary celebration! The temple stood brilliantly complete, surrounded by the children of Israel. The sounds of trumpets, cymbals, harps, lyres, and other instruments washed the air with music. Then, like a waterfall just within earshot, came the fresh but powerful sound of praise from people singing to the Lord: "He is good; his love endures forever." And God's presence, like a dense cloud, so filled the temple that the priests could not even do their work!

Question: When was the last time God's presence so filled your temple that you could not carry on your usual work?

Faithlift: You can celebrate the fact that this same God delights to make your heart His home.

June 4

If my people, who are called by my name, will humble themselves and pray and seek my face and turn from their wicked ways, then will I hear from heaven and will forgive their sin and will heal their land. 2 Chronicles 7:14

Further reading: 2 Chronicles 7:11–22

Shakespeare said, "What's in a name?" As children, many of us knew the adage "Sticks and stones may break my bones but words can never hurt me." But names do mark us; and labels tend to stick, making it all the more amazing that God would choose to give us His name. We know the names we deserve to be called, and "child of God" is not one of them!

Question: What name do you prefer to be called?

Faithlift: Thank God for giving you His good name.

June 5

All King Solomon's goblets were gold, and all the household articles in the Palace of the Forest of Lebanon were pure gold. Nothing was made of silver, because silver was considered of little value in Solomon's day. 2 Chronicles 9:20

Further reading: 2 Chronicles 9:13–28

Solomon's splendor outgrandeured any of the world's greatest kingdoms. Heads of state, high-ranking officials, merchants, and traders from around the world deposited gold and silver into Solomon's treasuries. "King Solomon was greater in riches and wisdom than all the other kings of the earth. All the kings of the earth sought audience with Solomon to hear the wisdom God had put in his heart. Year after year, everyone who came brought a gift—articles of silver and gold, and robes, weapons and spices, and horses and mules" (vv. 22–24).

Such surplus devalued silver and made it "as common in Jerusalem as stones" (v. 27). Kings did not pour into Jerusalem to see Solomon's splendor. Rather, they journeyed to hear Solomon's heart, a storehouse of wisdom from God. The true treasure of God's wisdom always devalues the world's trinkets and makes them as common as stones.

Question: Which are you seeking?

Faithlift: Be a storehouse of wisdom, not a stockpile of silver.

JUNE 6

After Rehoboam's position as king was established and he had become strong, he and all Israel with him abandoned the law of the LORD. 2 Chronicles 12:1

Further reading: 2 Chronicles 12:1–16

After King Solomon died, Rehoboam succeeded him as king of Israel. Like his father, he had many wives, concubines, sons, and daughters. It took focus and force to establish and strengthen his position as king, but at last he felt secure. To celebrate, he "abandoned the law of the LORD" (v. 1). The Bible doesn't say that Rehoboam called his activities celebration, but that is, in fact, what they were. Godly wisdom was not a genetic gift from his father Solomon. Rehoboam would have to ask for it, as his father had done. But Rehoboam chose instead to forsake God's laws and lead his people to do likewise. A sense of security dulled his sense of need for God's wisdom and his desire to obey God's laws. Security can do the same to us.

Question: Are you relying on genetics to do what only God can do?

Faithlift: Use your head; choose to obey God today.

JUNE 7

There was war between Abijah and Jeroboam. Abijah went into

battle with a force of four hundred thousand able fighting men, and Jeroboam drew up a battle line against him with eight hundred thousand able troops.
2 Chronicles 13:2–3

Further reading: 2 Chronicles 13

Abijah, son of Rehoboam and grandson of Solomon, assessed the sea of soldiers. The odds were two to one against him. He had four hundred thousand men, and Jeroboam's troops numbered eight hundred thousand. But Abijah possessed a not-so-secret weapon. God had given the land to David's descendants, and he was one of them. And Jeroboam, builder of golden calves, encourager of idol worship, and recruiter of anybody-will-do priests, must have shivered under his shining armor when Abijah's words hit their royal target. The most powerful volley followed. "We are observing the requirements of the LORD our God. But you have forsaken him. God is with us; he is our leader" (vv. 11–12). Jeroboam and his vast troops became casualties instead of conquerors.

Question: Where would you have placed your confidence?

Faithlift: Obey God and be a conqueror instead of a casualty.

JUNE 8

Then Asa called to the LORD his God and said, "LORD there is no one like you to help the powerless against the mighty. Help us, O LORD our God, for we rely on you, and in your name we have come against this vast army. O LORD, you are our God; do not let man prevail against you."
2 Chronicles 14:11

Further reading: 2 Chronicles 14

King Abijah died and his son, Asa, succeeded him as king of Judah. He did what was right in God's eyes, destroying former places of idol worship and commanding his people to seek God and obey His laws. The land and people rested under such wise leadership. Then the day came when the Cushites, an ungodly people, marched onto their turf and drew up battle lines. King Asa, hit with the unusual challenge of war, did the usual and called on his God for help. God, hearing Asa's familiar voice, answered and crushed the Cushites.

Question: How is your relationship with God when all is at rest?

Faithlift: There is no one like God to "help the powerless against the mighty."

JUNE 9

But as for you, be strong and do not give up, for your work will be rewarded. 2 Chronicles 15:7

Further reading: 2 Chronicles 15

God sent encouragement to King Asa through Azariah. Asa was reforming Judah and Benjamin through his search-and-destroy-all-idols mission. Asa even deposed his grandmother as queen mother, "because she had made a repulsive Asherah pole" (v. 16). To do right is tough and usually unpopular work, so Azariah must have been a welcome gift to Asa. We need more Asas and Azariahs around today—Asas to do right and Azariahs to encourage them never to give up. God will reward both.

Question: Which one would you choose to be?

Faithlift: "Be strong and do not give up, for your work will be rewarded."

JUNE 10

For the eyes of the LORD range throughout the earth to strengthen those whose hearts are fully committed to him. 2 Chronicles 16:9

Further reading: 2 Chronicles 16

Asa began his reign doing good in God's eyes. He brought about religious reforms, sought God eagerly, and encouraged his people to do the same. But in his last years he lowered his sights and made an alliance with a wicked king, buying him off with gold and silver from the temple treasuries. God, through a prophet, reminded Asa that He had a history of taking care of his people. God jarred Asa's memory with details of how He had delivered former enemies into their hands. "For the eyes of the LORD range throughout the earth to strengthen those whose hearts are fully committed to him." While Asa set his sights on a lesser alliance, God searched for a faithful heart that was fully committed to Him. God would give His strength to a faithful heart. But Asa's was not the one.

Question: Where have you set your sights?

Faithlift: God is looking to strengthen your faithful heart today.

June 11

But Jehoshaphat also said to the king of Israel, "First seek the counsel of the LORD."
2 Chronicles 18:4

Further reading: 2 Chronicles 18:1–27

Jehoshaphat, king of Judah, enjoyed wealth and honor and was devoted to God; but he was related to wicked King Ahab by marriage. Ahab asked Jehoshaphat to fight with him against Ramoth Gilead. Jehoshaphat agreed in principle but added, "First seek the counsel of the LORD." This was a new way of dealing for Ahab. But he called together the four hundred prophets, his yes men, who quickly agreed that Ahab and Jehoshaphat should go to war, for "God [would] give it into the king's hand" (v. 5). But Jehoshaphat persisted, "Is there not a prophet of the LORD here whom we can inquire of?" (v. 6) Jehoshaphat questioned the yes of the four hundred false prophets and insisted on truth from one man of God. Truth is worth the wait.

Question: Would you have accepted the majority report?

Faithlift: Dare to speak God's truth today.

June 12

O our God, will you not judge them? For we have no power to face this vast army that is attacking us. We do not know what to do, but our eyes are upon you. 2 *Chronicles 20:12*

Further reading: 2 Chronicles 20:1–30

Jehoshaphat, king of Judah, was standing before his people when he received word that a vast army was bearing down on them. As their leader, he modeled wisdom and faith in God. After the initial wave of alarm swept over him, Jehoshaphat "resolved to inquire of the LORD, and he proclaimed a fast for all Judah. The people of Judah came together to seek help from the LORD; indeed, they came from every town in Judah to seek Him" (vv. 3–4). Then King Jehoshaphat stood up and called on the Lord. His prayer reminded the people of God's faithfulness and power and underscored to God their powerlessness before such formidable troops. "We have no power to face this vast army that is attacking us. We do not know what to do, but our eyes are upon you." Such faith in God will never go unnoticed or unprotected.

Question: Where do you focus your eyes when you don't know what to do?

Faithlift: Resolve to look up and inquire of the Lord.

June 13

This is what the LORD says to you: "Do not be afraid or discouraged because of this vast army. For the battle is not yours, but God's." 2 *Chronicles 20:15*

Further reading: 2 Chronicles 20:1–30

King Jehoshaphat's faith quieted the quaking spirits of

his fearful people. They were alarmed to know that a vast army approached, but they were reassured to see their king's faith and to hear God's words of encouragement. "Do not be afraid or discouraged because of this vast army. For the battle is not yours, but God's."

Question: Are you exhausted from a battle that is not yours to fight?

Faithlift: Faith focuses on God, not on the enemy's army.

JUNE 14

You will not have to fight this battle. Take up your positions; stand firm and see the deliverance the LORD will give you, O Judah and Jerusalem. Do not be afraid; do not be discouraged. Go out to face them tomorrow, and the LORD will be with you.
2 Chronicles 20:17

Further reading: 2 Chronicles 20:1–30

It was easy for the Israelites to be full of faith when they were gathered inside the walls of Jerusalem, but tomorrow's faith needed legs strong enough to dig in and stand firm when flight was instinctive—legs steady enough to support bodies that took positions, faced the enemy, and believed what human eyes could not see: that the Lord was with them. There was no outward fight required for this war; only an inward battle of belief. What they chose to believe on the inside today would be visible to their world tomorrow.

Question: How fit are your faith's legs?

Faithlift: Faith gives you more than a leg to stand on.

JUNE 15

Jehoshaphat stood and said, . . . "Have faith in the LORD your God and you will be upheld; have faith in his prophets and you will be successful." After consulting the people, Jehoshaphat appointed

men to sing to the LORD and to praise him for the splendor of his holiness as they went out at the head of the army, saying: "Give thanks to the LORD, for his love endures forever." As they began to sing and praise, the LORD set ambushes against the men of Ammon and Moab and Mount Seir who were invading Judah, and they were defeated.
2 Chronicles 20:20–22

Further reading: 2 Chronicles 20:1–30

Can you imagine a manual on war that resembled a hymnal? Only faith sings when facing such formidable odds! While the children of Israel sang, their enemies slaughtered each other. By the time they had reached the battlefield, "they saw only dead bodies lying on the ground; no one had escaped. So Jehoshaphat and his men went to carry off their plunder, and they found among them a great amount of equipment and clothing and also articles of value—more than they could take away" (vv. 24–25). But their faith had allowed them to sing before they saw the slain bodies or the plunder. That's faith for you!

Question: Are you willing to do battle armed with faith in God and a song?

Faithlift: Faith sings before it sees.

JUNE 16

And the kingdom of Jehoshaphat was at peace, for his God had given him rest on every side.
2 Chronicles 20:30

Further reading: 2 Chronicles 20:1–30

Such total defeat of Judah's enemies did not go unnoticed by those who had hoped to overtake them. Can't you hear folks talk! "You mean to tell me all they did was sing? That must have been some song to send the enemy into such confusion that they killed each other!" But it was more than a song. Soldiers have sung war tunes before and have drilled and marched to tuneful beats. This song bore no cadence to help the Israelites step lively. This tune lifted God's heart, not man's feet. That's why fear fell on the surrounding kingdoms. The fear of the Lord said, "Don't even think about it!" They didn't, and peace fell on Jehoshaphat and Judah.

Question: How at peace is your kingdom?

Faithlift: The peace of God follows the songs of faith.

JUNE 17

Jehoram was thirty-two years old when he became king, and he reigned in Jerusalem eight years. He passed away, to no one's regret, and was buried in the City of David, but not in the tombs of the kings. 2 Chronicles 21:20

Further reading: 2 Chronicles 21

Jehoshaphat had ruled Judah with wisdom. Now his son, Jehoram, succeeded him as king. "He did evil in the eyes of the LORD" (v. 6). He turned away from the Lord and led his people to do the same. Jehoram rebuilt the high places where they worshiped other gods. Elijah the prophet said of him, "You have also murdered your own brothers, members of your father's house, men who were better than you" (v. 13). Jehoram's choices brought him God's punishment and a tragic epitaph: "He passed away, to no one's regret."

Question: What would you like written about you?

Faithlift: Our choices determine our epitaph.

JUNE 18

Ahaziah was twenty-two years old when he became king, and he reigned in Jerusalem one year. His mother's name was Athaliah, a granddaughter of Omri. He too walked in the ways of the house of Ahab, for his mother encouraged him in doing wrong. 2 Chronicles 22:2–3

Further reading: 2 Chronicles 22

Parents have a powerful influence on children, no matter what their age.

Question: How are you using the influence you have?

Faithlift: God, your Father, empowers and encourages you to do good.

JUNE 19

He did what was right in the eyes of the LORD, but not wholeheartedly. 2 Chronicles 25:2

Further reading: 2 Chronicles 25

Amaziah, another king of Judah, was not so amazing. He's not unlike a lot of us who "do what's right in the eyes of the LORD, but not wholeheartedly." There's no heart in half a heart. God is looking for people who will love and obey Him with all their heart.

Question: Are you one of them?

Faithlift: Put your whole heart into this day with God.

JUNE 20

In the eighth year of his reign, while he was still young, he began to seek the God of his father David. 2 Chronicles 34:3

Further reading: 2 Chronicles 34

Josiah became king of Judah when he was eight years old. "He did what was right in the eyes of the LORD and walked in the ways of his father David, not turning aside to the right or to the left" (v. 2). In his eighth year as king, sixteen-year-old Josiah "began to seek the God of his father David." God had been with Josiah as an eight-year-old child-king. But the older he grew, the more Josiah had to decide if he was on God's side. We know that at sixteen he decided "to seek the God of his father David." Josiah ruled as one tough teen! What a great example to people of all ages, then and now.

Question: Have you decided to seek God with your whole heart?

Faithlift: There is no age limit for those who seek God.

JUNE 21

These searched for their family records, but they could not find them and so were excluded from the priesthood as unclean.
Ezra 2:62

Further reading: Ezra 2:1–2, 61–70

A materialistic culture such as ours manufactures clutter. It's easy to misplace important items when surrounded by trivial ones. Perhaps too many of us can identify with these would-be priests. They had been in captivity for many years—not the best of living situations. Now, free of Babylonian bondage, they were ready to serve but lacked the necessary papers. The documents had been lost somewhere in captivity. No one had missed them until today, when they were called on to serve. No papers? No priests.

Question: Is clutter keeping you from more important matters?

Faithlift: God, who ordered the universe, can help you bring order to your world.

JUNE 22

No one could distinguish the sound of the shouts of joy from the sound of weeping, because the people made so much noise. And the sound was heard far away.
Ezra 3:13

Further reading: Ezra 3

What sights and sounds bombarded heaven that day! Like freed hostages, God's children, back home in Jerusalem, began rebuilding the temple. The foundation was laid, and shouts of praise ascended to God. But tired old eyes remembered another day and a magnificent temple where now only a foundation lay, and they wept. Others, born and raised in captivity, knew only stories about the temple in Jerusalem, so they shouted for joy at the sight of a new beginning. "No one could distinguish the sound of the shouts of joy from the sound of weeping, because the people made so much noise. And the sound was heard far away." There are no shouts or sobs that go unnoticed in heaven.

Question: When was the last time you shouted for joy?

Faithlift: Your shouts for joy and your sobs are heard in heaven today.

JUNE 23

Then the peoples around them set out to discourage the people of Judah and make them afraid to go on building. They hired counselors to work against them and frustrate their plans. Ezra 4:4–5

Further reading: Ezra 4–6:2

The enemies of God and His children, hearing the sounds of joy and weeping, stirred the pot of opposition brewing against the children of Israel. God had moved the heart of Cyrus, king of Persia, who had thus encouraged God's children to return to Jerusalem to rebuild the temple (see Ezra 1). They had begun the work but now experienced spirited opposition from their neighbors, who "set out to discourage the people of Judah and make them afraid to go on building." They picked and plotted and entangled them in official red tape until "the work on the house of God in Jerusalem came to a standstill until the second year of the reign of Darius king of Persia" (v. 24). They could only stop it "*Until.*" God allowed a pause, not a permanent shutdown. God's the keeper of the clock, as the enemies of God and His children came to learn when the rebuilding resumed.

Question: Can you recall a time when you encountered professional discouragers?

Faithlift: Praise the God who controls the "until"—who allows a pause, then proceeds to the finish.

JUNE 24

For seven days they celebrated with joy the Feast of the Unleavened Bread, because the LORD had filled them with joy by changing the attitude of the king of Assyria, so that he assisted them in the work on the house of God, the God of Israel. Ezra 6:22

Further reading: Ezra 6

God's persistent children had faced multiple forms of opposition to the rebuilding of the temple. One king had decreed yes; another had halted their work. But during the second year of his reign King Darius of Persia encouraged their work—with pay! Some of the king's officials sought to block the building of the temple with an assortment of intimidations: Who authorized you? and what are your names? These plucky, persistent Jews responded, "We are the servants of the God of heaven and earth, and we are rebuilding the temple that was built many years ago. . . . King Cyrus issued a decree to rebuild this house. . . . Now if it pleases the king, let a search be made in the royal archives of Babylon to see if King Cyrus did in fact issue a decree to rebuild this house of God in Jerusalem. Then let the king send us his decision in this matter" (Ezra 5:11, 13, 17). The search substantiated their claims and stirred the king to add, "Do not interfere with the work on this temple of God . . . moreover, . . . the expenses of these men are to be fully paid out of the royal treasury. . . . Whatever is needed . . . for burnt offerings to the God of heaven, . . . as requested by the priests in Jerusalem—must be given them daily without fail, so that they may offer sacrifices pleasing to the God of heaven and pray for the well-being of the king and his sons" (vv. 7–10). No wonder God's children celebrated joyfully for seven days!

Question: In what areas do you need to have that kind of persistence?

Faithlift: Persist and prepare to celebrate.

JUNE 25

I was ashamed to ask the king for soldiers and horsemen to protect us from enemies on the road, because we had told the king, "The good hand of our God is on everyone who looks to him, but his great anger is against all who forsake him." So we fasted and petitioned our God about this, and he answered our prayer. Ezra 8:22–23

Further reading: Ezra 7–8

Powerful King Artaxerxes granted permission to Ezra, priest and teacher of God's law, to take all willing Israelites with him to Jerusalem. He gave his blessing and provisions from the royal treasury and would have given whatever else Ezra needed to guarantee the safe return of the exiled Israelites. But Ezra neither took nor gave advantage to this mighty monarch. He had lived long enough to know that God had been and would always be their real savior. It must have been tempting to ask for the king's protection, but more was at stake than their lives. Ezra had proclaimed God's protection: "The good hand of our God is on everyone who looks to him," so he replaced his understandable fear with a fast. "We fasted and petitioned our God about this, and he answered our prayer." We need to feel more of Ezra's shame at requesting of others what God plans to do. Good example, Ezra!

Question: Is there something you're asking of someone that God wants to do for you?

Faithlift: Put your expectations on God and enjoy watching Him answer your prayers.

JUNE 26

O my God, I am too ashamed and disgraced to lift up my face to you, my God, because our sins are higher than our heads and our guilt has reached to the heavens. Ezra 9:6

Further reading: Ezra 9

The leaders of Israel came to Ezra to inform him that "the people of Israel, including the priests and the Levites, ha[d] not kept themselves separate from the neighboring peoples with their detestable practices . . . they ha[d] taken some of their daughters as wives for themselves and their sons, and ha[d] mingled the holy race with the peoples around them. And the leaders and officials ha[d] led the way in this unfaithfulness" (vv. 1–2). When Ezra heard this, he tore his tunic, pulled hair from his head and beard, sat down appalled until the evening sacrifice (see vv. 3–4), and then fell to his knees and prayed for *our* sins. Such identification with the sins of others encouraged a large group of Israelites to weep and repent as well. We need to decrease our finger pointing and increase our fasting and praying.

Question: Are you more of a pointer or a prayer?

Faithlift: Prayer uses your fingers for a higher purpose.

June 27

When I heard these things, I sat down and wept. For some days I mourned and fasted and prayed before the God of heaven.
Nehemiah 1:4

Further reading: Nehemiah 1

What makes you weep? Nehemiah, cupbearer for King Artaxerxes, received this word about the survivors of the Babylonian exile and status of Jerusalem: "Those who survived the exile and are back in the province are in great trouble and disgrace. The wall of Jerusalem is broken down, and its gates have been burned with fire" (v. 3). Such news made Nehemiah sit down and weep. His personal status and security did not dull his sensitivities to brothers and sisters in need. He did not forget his people, although they were far away.

Question: What makes you weep?

Faithlift: Treasure a sensitive spirit more than status and security.

June 28

I was very much afraid, but I said to the king, "May the king live forever! Why should my face not look sad when the city where my fathers are buried lies in ruins, and its gates have been destroyed by fire?" Nehemiah 2:2–3

Further reading: Nehemiah 2:1–10

Nehemiah's countenance caught the king's attention. His usual disposition must have been pleasant as he performed his duties as the king's cupbearer; otherwise, his sad face would not have caused King Artaxerxes to inquire of Nehemiah, "Why does your face look so sad when you are not ill? This can be nothing but sadness of heart" (v. 2). Nehemiah, fearful but focused on Jerusalem, answered the king at great personal risk. And God protected His courageous cupbearer.

Question: How willing are you to take risks on behalf of others?

Faithlift: Faith doesn't let fear dictate the dialogue or the day's events.

June 29

The king said to me, "What is it you want?" Then I prayed to the God of heaven, and I answered the king. Nehemiah 2:4–5

Further reading: Nehemiah 2:1–10

Nehemiah didn't have time to drop to his knees in prayer. This was a walk-and-talk prayer. The king asked and Nehemiah answered, but not before he "prayed to the God of heaven." Nehemiah's heart, not his circumstances, determined his winning sequence: caring, praying, then speaking.

Question: What do you want that needs God's help?

Faithlift: Dare to ask for something big enough to need God's assistance.

June 30

The next section was repaired by the men of Tekoa, but their nobles would not put their shoulders to the work under their supervisors. Nehemiah 3:5

Further reading: Nehemiah 2:11–3:5

Nehemiah inspected the ruins of Jerusalem's walls, then instructed and motivated the people to rebuild. While some government officials mocked and ridiculed them, God's children continued rebuilding. We can read of section after section of the wall being repaired by a group or family, then comes the section being repaired by the men of Tekoa. "But their nobles would not put their shoulders to the work under their supervisors." There's nothing noble about neglecting your duty.

Question: How would you have motivated the nobles to do their part?

Faithlift: It's nobler to shoulder your load.

July

July 1

They all plotted together to come and fight against Jerusalem and stir up trouble against it. But we prayed to our God and posted a guard day and night to meet this threat. Nehemiah 4:8–9

Further reading: Nehemiah 4:1–15

There will always be enemies who are angry and incensed that God's work is progressing. Nehemiah and a remnant of persistent Jews endured constant insults designed to discourage them from rebuilding the wall. But while the enemy plotted, Nehemiah and his team prayed and posted guards day and night. The enemy's cleverest plots were no match for the prayers and posted guards of God's children. Meanwhile, the wall grew, as did the faith of Nehemiah and his tough team.

Question: How do you meet the threats that come to discourage you from finishing your work?

Faithlift: Praying and posting guards encourages a strong finish.

July 2

Don't be afraid of them. Remember the Lord, who is great and awesome, and fight for your brothers, your sons and your daughters, your wives and your homes. Nehemiah 4:14

Further reading: Nehemiah 4

The frustrated enemies of God's children increased their threats as the wall grew. Nehemiah rallied his people behind a call to focus on God. His challenge, simply stated, was to fear God, not the enemy, and fight for their families. The Israelites needed to be reminded that they were constructing more than a wall. So do we.

Question: Where is your focus?

Faithlift: "Remember the Lord, who is great and awesome."

JULY 3

They kept quiet, because they could find nothing to say.
Nehemiah 5:8

Further reading: Nehemiah 5:1–13

Sometimes the enemy is within our own ranks. While most Jews worked hard on the wall, others busily enslaved their countrymen through usury. When Nehemiah heard the outcry of the poor, his anger burned at these Jews who had taken advantage of their own people. He pondered the charges against the greedy lot, then accused the guilty nobles and officials. "You are exacting usury from your own countrymen! . . . As far as possible, we have bought back our Jewish brothers who were sold to the Gentiles. Now you are selling your brothers, only for them to be sold back to us!" (vv. 7–8) These wicked Jews knew Nehemiah spoke the truth, so "they kept quiet, because they could find nothing to say." Nehemiah went on to demand that they make restitution to the poor they had exploited. "'We will give it back,' they said, 'and we will not demand anything more from them. We will do as you say'" (v. 12). And they kept their promise.

Question: How do you respond when hit with a tough truth?

Faithlift: Wisdom knows when to speak and when to remain silent.

JULY 4

Their assistants also lorded it over the people. But out of reverence for God I did not act like that. Instead, I devoted myself to the work on this wall.
Nehemiah 5:15–16

Further reading: Nehemiah 5:14–19

Nehemiah, a strong but sensitive leader, resisted his predecessors' demanding, demeaning lifestyles. This leader exacted no food, wine, or burdensome taxes from his countrymen. Instead, he "devoted [himself] to the work on the wall." Nehemiah relinquished what rightfully belonged to a man in his position. Then this extraordinary leader prayed, "Remember me with favor, O my God, for all I have done for these people" (v. 19). How God must love to remember leaders like Nehemiah who refuse riches and power out of reverence for God and His children.

Question: What would you like God to remember you for?

Faithlift: Refuse some riches out of reverence for God and love for His children.

JULY 5

[Nehemiah replied,] "I am carrying on a great project and cannot go down. Why should the work stop while I leave it and go down to you?" Nehemiah 6:3

Further reading: Nehemiah 6:1–14

Squeaky hinges like Sanballat, Tobiah, and Geshem nibble at our attention. Unchecked, they divert us from our greater projects. Nehemiah was no stranger to these diversionary tactics, so he resisted their schemes to lure him from completing the final touches on the wall. To their messengers Nehemiah responded, "I am carrying on a great project and cannot go down. Why should the work stop while I leave it and go down to you?" It's too easy to oil the loudest hinge and miss completing the quiet but greater work.

Question: How easily distracted are you?

Faithlift: God's power enables us to tune out the squeaky hinges and focus on the greater project.

July 6

They were all trying to frighten us, thinking, "Their hands will get too weak for the work, and it will not be completed." But I prayed, "Now strengthen my hands." Nehemiah 6:9

Further reading: Nehemiah 6:1–16

Fear weakens our spirits and our bodies. When our hearts are defeated, our bodies surrender without a fight. While the enemies of God's children and His work continued to set roadblocks, Nehemiah set his heart upon finishing the great project. When he failed to halt the wall with intimidating messages, Sanballat attacked the Israelites' motives. "It is reported among the nations—and Geshem says it is true—that you and the Jews are plotting to revolt, and therefore you are building the wall. Moreover, according to these reports you are about to become their king and have even appointed prophets to make this proclamation about you in Jerusalem: 'There is a king in Judah!' Now this report will get back to the king; so come, let us confer together" (vv. 6–7). Insults, threats, and lies combined to peck the life out of Nehemiah. But he prepared for battle, not with clenched fists, but with folded hands. Nehemiah prayed, "Now strengthen my hands" (v. 9). And God strengthened His prayerful warrior.

Question: How are you handling those who seek to derail or discredit you?

Faithlift: Hands folded in prayer are more than a match for the clenched fists you face today.

July 7

So the wall was completed on the twenty-fifth of Elul, in fifty-two days. When all our enemies heard about this and all the surrounding nations saw it, our enemies lost their self-confidence, because they realized that this work had been done with the help of our God. Nehemiah 6:15–16

Further reading: Nehemiah 6:1–16

We seem to be able to do too much of our work without God's help. We experience little or no interference from God's enemies, however, because our projects are insignificant. When we get involved with God-sized projects, enemy attacks mount. Nehemiah, involved in a God-sized project, faced full-scale war. But God won in the end. The wall stood complete, a testimony to the faith and perseverance of Nehemiah, a remnant of Jews, and to their great God. Whenever the enemies saw the wall, they were reminded of the tenacity of these Jews and the triumph of their God. Thus, they "lost their self-confidence" and, ultimately, the war.

Question: How necessary is God to the completion of your projects?

Faithlift: Stretch your faith through a God-sized project.

JULY 8

So on the first day of the seventh month Ezra the priest brought the Law before the assembly, which was made up of men and women and all who were able to understand. He read it aloud from daybreak till noon as he faced the square before the Water Gate in the presence of the men, women and others who could understand. And all the people listened attentively to the Book of the Law. Nehemiah 8:2–3

Further reading: Nehemiah 8

Like parched pilgrims, God's children lapped up the law of God. They drank, not because the law was tasty, but because it was vital. Real life grew out of obedience to the law. However, they had to know the law in order to do it. So Ezra read aloud to God's thirsty children, not for a few minutes, like many church services, but "from daybreak till noon." The people stood while he read, "listen[ing] attentively to the Book of the Law." When we are thirsty and find living water, we drink.

Question: How are you quenching your thirst?

Faithlift: God's words, heard and obeyed, bring health to body and soul.

JULY 9

"This day is sacred to the LORD *your God. Do not mourn or weep." For all the people had been weeping as they listened to the words of the Law. Nehemiah 8:9*

Further reading: Nehemiah 8

The Israelites' starved souls reacted to this feast of words. God's Words reminded, convicted, and instructed them, resonating with their deepest longings to know and love God. Understandably, they mourned and wept. But wise Nehemiah turned their focus from sorrow to joy. "Go and enjoy choice food and sweet drinks, and send some to those who have nothing prepared. This day is sacred to our Lord. Do not grieve, for the joy of the LORD is your strength" (v. 10). There would be times of confession, but today was a day for celebration. These faithful few who stood inside the freshly walled Jerusalem, feeding on God's words, caused celebration in heaven as well as in Jerusalem!

Question: Are you enjoying God's celebrations?

Faithlift: Celebrate! God's joy is your strength today.

JULY 10

On the twenty-fourth day of the same month, the Israelites gathered together, fasting and wearing sackcloth and having dust on their heads. . . . They stood in their places and confessed their sins and the wickedness of their fathers. Nehemiah 9:1–2

Further reading: Nehemiah 9

There are seasons of celebration and seasons of repentance. This season of celebration prepared the soil for a season of confession. God's children felt overwhelmed by the sins of their fathers as well as their own sins. Confession, not blame, poured from their mouths. As they scanned the decades, listened to their painful histories, and heard the law's demands, God's children identified with past sinners and repented.

Question: Is it time for us to stand in our places and confess?

Faithlift: Knowing and loving God results in seasons of confession as well as celebration.

JULY 11

But see, we are slaves today, slaves in the land you gave our forefathers so they could eat its fruit and the other good things it produces. Because of our sins, its abundant harvest goes to the kings you have placed over us.
Nehemiah 9:36–37

Further reading: Nehemiah 9

God's children stood long, for their confessions were many. Their cries and prayers contrasted God's faithfulness with their own history of rebellion. Like the ocean's relentless waves came recollections of God's compassion and repeated deliverance through decades of their unfaithfulness. The final wave pounded them with the bitter truth: "We are slaves today, slaves in the land you gave our forefathers so they could eat its fruit and the other good things it produces. *Because of our sins,* its abundant harvest goes to the kings you have placed over us" (emphasis added). How painful to face our sins and realize what we have allowed to be stolen from us under the guise of freedom or pleasure! But what greater joy to confess, repent, and receive God's forgiveness. We can begin afresh and be set free!

Question: Is there an area where you are still a slave?

Faithlift: God wants you free to enjoy His harvest.

JULY 12

And on that day they offered great sacrifices, rejoicing because God had given them great joy. The women and children also rejoiced. The sound of rejoicing in Jerusalem could be heard far away. Nehemiah 12:43

Further reading: Nehemiah 12:27–47

The days of confession made sweeter the time of celebration. God's children gathered again; but this time music, not mourning filled the air. They had come to dedicate the wall. Sounds of choirs, lyres, harps, and cymbals replaced the sounds of construction. Some outsiders who were far away from the site of celebration and the Source of joy probably heard the music and licked dry lips, longing for a sip from the Spring of such joy.

Question: Could you have led them to the Spring? Would you?

Faithlift: Share a sip of Living Water today.

JULY 13

In the thirty-second year of Artaxerxes king of Babylon I had returned to the king.
Nehemiah 13:6

Further reading: Nehemiah 13

Nehemiah, cupbearer for King Artaxerxes, left Babylon in the twentieth year of his reign to build the wall in Jerusalem (see Nehemiah 2:1). He returned twelve years later. Who bore the cup in the meantime? Who stepped in so Nehemiah could step out for a dozen years? Whoever filled in participated in something greater than wine tasting. (That was the cupbearer's job—to take the first drink to check for poison.) Nehemiah's replacement aligned himself with God's purposes to care for His children. Eventually, Nehemiah returned to Babylon. With the great wall completed, he resumed a life of routine and daily duty that challenges our desire and need to live by faith.

Question: How much faith is required for your daily routine?

Faithlift: Thank God for those who fill in and help fulfill God's purposes for you and others.

JULY 14

And who knows but that you have come to royal position for such a time as this? Esther 4:14

Further reading: Esther 1–4

King Xerxes ruled vast territories but not his own household. He banished his strong-minded queen and brought forward Esther as Queen Vashti's replacement. Unknown to the king, however, his beautiful new bride was Jewish. Haman, honored official in the king's court, despised Jews, especially Esther's uncle, Mordecai. So Haman plotted to destroy all the Jews. When Mordecai learned of the plot, he sent word to Esther asking her to beg the king for mercy for her people. Esther replied that she would risk death if she approached the king uninvited, but Mordecai responded, "Do not think that because you are in the king's house you alone of all the Jews will escape. For if you remain silent at this time, relief and deliverance for the Jews will arise from another place, but you and your father's family will perish. And who knows but that you have come to royal position for such a time as this?" (vv. 13–14). Esther listened to her uncle and acted on his wisdom. Mordecais and Esthers—people who speak and do the truth despite personal risk—are too few in our culture.

Question: Has God placed you somewhere unique "for such a time as this"?

Faithlift: Dare to speak and do truth where God has placed you, "for such a time as this."

JULY 15

I'm the only person Queen Esther invited to accompany the king to the banquet she gave.

And she has invited me along with the king tomorrow. But all this gives me no satisfaction as long as I see that Jew Mordecai sitting at the king's gate.
Esther 5:12–13

Further reading: Esther 3–5

Haughty Haman churned at Mordecai's repeated refusal to bow down to him. Like a snake, Haman wriggled his way into the king and hissed his hatred for the Jews. "It is not in the king's best interest to tolerate them. If it pleases the king, let a decree be issued to destroy them" (3:8–9). The unwary king issued the decree and set in motion a chain of events that, without God's help, would have destroyed the Jews and left hateful Haman higher up in the king's court. But God intervened through a fearless uncle and his favorite niece. Slick Haman thought Esther favored him when she invited him to dine with the king. But his hatred for Mordecai left a continued bad taste in his mouth, making it impossible for him to enjoy his seeming good fortune. To make himself feel better, Haman built a seventy-five foot gallows from which to hang one small Jew named Mordecai. But God had another plan. When Esther informed the king of Haman's treachery, the king said, "'Hang him on it!' So they hanged Haman on the gallows he had prepared for Mordecai" (7:9–10). Hate has a way of hanging the hater instead of the hated.

Question: Are you hanging on to hatred?

Faithlift: Forgiveness gets rid of the bad taste hatred leaves in our mouths and our spirits.

JULY 16

Mordecai left the king's presence wearing royal garments of blue and white, a large crown of gold and a purple robe of fine linen. And the city of Susa held a joyous celebration. For the Jews it was a time of happiness and joy, gladness and honor.
Esther 8:15–16

Further reading: Esther 7–8

Mordecai the hated became Mordecai the honored, and Haman's hatred brought about his own death. The day before Haman died, the honor he had thought was his fell to Mordecai. The king even ordered Haman to get "the robe and the horse. He robed Mordecai, and led him on horseback through the city streets, proclaiming before him, 'This is what is done for the man the king delights to honor!'"(6:11) Mordecai the honored pulled by Haman the horse. But Mordecai's peace depended on the salvation of the Jews, not on the humiliation or destruction of Haman. So even after Haman's death, Mordecai and Esther moved to save the Jews from annihilation. The king turned to Mordecai to write another decree on behalf of the Jews and gave him the royal signet ring as the official seal of approval. What a turn of events! A despised Jew, wearing sackcloth and ashes and wailing for his people (see Esther 4:1–4), ended up donning royal robes and rejoicing with them. Only God works like that!

Question: Can you recall a time when God reversed a situation for your good?

Faithlift: This same God watches over you!

July 17

Mordecai the Jew was second in rank to King Xerxes, preeminent among the Jews, and held in high esteem by his many fellow Jews, because he worked for the good of his people and spoke up for the welfare of all the Jews.
Esther 10:3

Further reading: Esther 8–10

God's man Mordecai, a Jew from the tribe of Benjamin, knew the sting of minority status. Many years earlier Nebuchadnezzar had carried his family into captivity, where they remained to this day. Who would have dreamed that two despised Jews could rise to such places of prominence—Esther as queen and her uncle Mordecai second only to King Xerxes? Perhaps the greater miracle, however, is their ongoing sensitivity to their fellow Jews. It's easy to forget our roots when transplanted to a spectacular garden. Mordecai and Esther remembered and Jews hold them in high esteem to this day.

Question: Who is counting on you to remember them?

Faithlift: God will never forget you.

July 18

In the land of Uz there lived a man whose name was Job. This man was blameless and upright; he feared God and shunned evil. Job 1:1

Further reading: Job 1

Satan, the enemy of God and His children, returned from prowling the earth and challenged God concerning His child Job. God loved Job and told Satan, "There is no one on earth like him; he is blameless and upright, a man who fears God and shuns evil" (v. 8). The enemy retorted, "Does Job fear God for nothing? . . . Have you not put a hedge around him and his household and everything he has? You have blessed the work of his hands, so that his flocks and herds are spread throughout the land. But stretch out your hand and strike everything he has, and he will surely curse you to your face" (vv. 9–11). And "the LORD said to Satan, 'Very well, then, everything he has is in your hands, but on the man himself do not lay a finger'" (v. 12). How confident God was that Job's goodness was rooted in love for God and not in his love for God's blessings.

Question: Do you "fear God for nothing"?

Faithlift: God loves you "for nothing."

July 19

[Job] said: "Naked I came from my mother's womb, and naked I

will depart. The LORD gave and the LORD has taken away; may the name of the LORD be praised." In all this, Job did not sin by charging God with wrong-doing. Job 1:21–22

Further reading: Job 1

Not long after Satan and God conversed regarding Job, the attackers swooped down on Job and his family. Enemies stole his donkeys and camels and killed his servants; fires destroyed sheep and servants; and winds destroyed his house and ten children. With unrelenting fury the enemy beat at Job's faith by destroying the stuff of his life: people and possessions. Yet Job maintained his faith in God. What a shock to Satan and his enemy agents! But Job's faith did not surprise his God.

Question: Unlike Job, are you blaming God?

Faithlift: God is not your enemy.

JULY 20

When Job's three friends, Eliphaz the Temanite, Bildad the Shuhite and Zophar the Naamathite, heard about all the troubles that had come upon him, they set out from their homes and met together by agreement to go and sympathize with him and comfort him. When they saw him from a distance, they could hardly recognize him; they began to weep aloud, and they tore their robes and sprinkled dust on their heads. Then they sat on the ground with him for seven days and seven nights. No one said a word to him, because they saw how great his suffering was. Job 2:11–13

Further reading: Job 2

Some of God's best comforters simply sit with you in silence.

Question: Who needs your silent presence?

Faithlift: God sits with you in your silent suffering.

July 21

But if it were I, I would appeal to God; I would lay my cause before him. He performs wonders that cannot be fathomed, miracles that cannot be counted. Job 5:8–9

Further reading: Job 4–5

Job's friends could not remain silent. Eventually they spoke, but some of their words would better have been left unsaid. To this day unduly negative and judgmental advice from friends marks them as "Job's comforters." In Job 16:2 Job calls these friends "miserable comforters." But in the middle of many words were hidden some nuggets like gold in deep crevices. Words such as those spoken by Job's friend Eliphaz, "If it were I, I would appeal to God; I would lay my cause before him. He performs wonders that cannot be fathomed, miracles that cannot be counted," brought true comfort in times of deep despair.

Question: Have you known the comfort of this truth?

Faithlift: Miracles and wonders are the ordinary stuff of God's day.

July 22

I have become a laughingstock to my friends, though I called upon God and he answered—a mere laughingstock, though righteous and blameless! Men at ease have contempt for misfortune as the fate of those whose feet are slipping. The tents of marauders are undisturbed, and those who provoke God are secure—those who carry their god in their hands. Job 12:4–6

Further reading: Job:11–12

How many men and women have identified with Job through the ages! You may be wrestling with a variation on the theme of bad things happening to good people. Some of God's seemingly faithful, humble children have suffered enormous pain, disappointment, ridicule, and loss. You may look around and see injustice: God-haters prospering, thieves promoted, hedonists physically healthy. You may see thriving children and happy marriages among people who carry their gods in their billfolds. Job saw it, too, but somehow in the middle of multiplied misfortune, Job also maintained perspective on himself and his God. Instead of cursing God, he called on Him one more time.

Question: Do you carry your god or does your God carry you?

Faithlift: Call on the God who carries you.

July 23

What you know, I also know; I am not inferior to you. If only you would be altogether silent! For you, that would be wisdom. Job 13:2, 5

Further reading: Job: 4–13

Job's friends, like many of us, relied too heavily on words. Wisdom and words are not synonymous. We often inadvertently belittle our suffering friends by telling them what they already know. Sometimes our words become the primary source of suffering for a spouse, child, or friend. We all have the right to speak or to remain silent. Let us pray for wisdom to know when to speak.

Question: How heavily do you rely on words to instruct, correct, or encourage?

Faithlift: Wisdom knows when words can wait.

July 24

Though he slay me, yet will I hope in him. Job 13:15

Further reading: Job 12–13

Blistered, beaten, and belittled Job staked his life, now and hereafter, on God. His possessions, children, social standing, and health had vanished. Job's body, "clothed with worms and scabs, . . . broken and festering" (7:5), black and peeling and burning with fever (see 30:30), cried less than his tormented spirit. Yet even in the midst of torture Job trusted in God. And throughout history men, women, and children of God who have suffered torture for their faith have exclaimed, "Though he slay me, yet will I hope in him." What a holy heritage!

Question: Will you continue to trust?

Faithlift: Through testing, keep trusting.

JULY 25

I also could speak like you, if you were in my place; I could make fine speeches against you and shake my head at you. But my mouth would encourage you; comfort from my lips would bring you relief. Job 16:4–5

Further reading: Job:15–16

Job's choice confronts us daily. Some people provoke us to exchange blow for blow, gossip for gossip, curse for curse, rebuke for rebuke. To speak as Job's comforters spoke requires no wisdom or strength from God. That kind of speech comes naturally. But if we choose to use our words to encourage and comfort, we will need supernatural strength. God is ready when you are.

Question: How much encouragement comes from your lips?

Faithlift: Let God refresh others through your words.

JULY 26

Then Job replied: "How long will you torment me and crush me with words?" Job 19:1–2

Further reading: Job 18–19

Job's friends pelted him with unrelenting words. Like torrential rains on parched soil, their words gouged deep gullies. Job attempted to escape like a tired swimmer, only to be crushed with a fresh wave of words. His comforters rapped him with anger, guilt, idle chatter, ignorance, and faulty conclusions. And he remained crushed instead of wrapped in comfort.

Question: Do your words rain down comfort?

Faithlift: Love chooses to cover instead of condemn.

JULY 27

Oh, that my words were recorded, that they were written on a scroll. Job 19:23

Further reading: Job 19

They were, Job. They were.

Question: Would you want your words recorded?

Faithlift: God recorded Job's words to instruct and encourage us.

JULY 28

I know that my Redeemer lives, and that in the end he will stand upon the earth. And after my skin has been destroyed, yet in my flesh I will see God; I myself will see him with my own eyes—I, and not another. How my heart yearns within me! Job 19:25–27

Further reading: Job 19

Job knew the futility of trust in friends, health, status, and material wealth. He had watched seemingly sure things disappear. But two truths remained unshakable. Job's Redeemer lived, and Job would see Him one day with his own eyes. Those truths made his unbearable life bearable.

Question: Do you know the God who will stand when all else has fallen?

Faithlift: Put your trust in unshakable truths: your Redeemer lives, and one day you will see Him face to face.

JULY 29

I have not departed from the commands of his lips; I have treasured the words of his mouth

more than my daily bread.
Job 23:12

Further reading: Job 23

There would be less obesity of heart, head, and body if we treasured God's words "more than our daily bread."

Question: Which diet would you thrive on?

Faithlift: Give us this day your living bread, O God.

JULY 30

Men listened to me expectantly, waiting in silence for my counsel. After I had spoken, they spoke no more; my words fell gently on their ears. They waited for me as for showers and drank in my words as the spring rain. When I smiled at them, they scarcely believed it; the light of my face was precious to them.
Job 29:21–24

Further reading: Job 29–30

Job's pain intensified with vivid rememberings. His past honors increased his present humiliation. In months gone by Job's speech and smile had refreshed those he had encountered like gentle spring showers. Now some of these same folks peppered him with insults, spit on his once smiling face, and mocked him in song. Once upon a time Job had refreshed others; now, he repulsed them. They preferred winners. So do we.

Question: How do you respond to losers?

Faithlift: God loves losers.

JULY 31

Brace yourself like a man; I will question you, and you shall answer me. Where were you when I laid the earth's foundation? . . . Have you entered the storehouses of the snow or seen the storehouses of the hail, which I reserve for times of trouble . . . ? Who endowed the heart with wisdom or gave understanding to the mind? Who has the wisdom to count the clouds? Who can tip over the water jars of the heavens when the dust becomes hard and the

clods of earth stick together?
Job 38:3, 4, 22, 36–38

Further reading: Job 32–42

The time came when man's words—both Job's and his friends'—ceased. They sat completely spent, empty of words and wisdom. Then God whipped pictures through a whirlwind. Rhetorical questions and masterpiece descriptions challenged their assumptions, erased their arguments, and lifted their focus from one creature and life's injustices to the Creator of all. Something happened to Job as he sat and listened. God washed Job's world in awe as the Creator and His creation stopped to communicate.

Question: When was the last time you sat and really communicated with your Creator?

Faithlift: Listen. God wants to communicate with you.

AUGUST

AUGUST 1

Then Job replied to the LORD: "I know that you can do all things; no plan of yours can be thwarted. You asked, 'Who is this that obscures my counsel without knowledge?' Surely I spoke of things I did not understand, things too wonderful for me to know. You said, 'Listen now, and I will speak; I will question you, and you shall answer me.' My ears had heard of you but now my eyes have seen you. Therefore, I despise myself and repent in dust and ashes." Job 42:1–6

Further reading: Job 40–42

While God's words penetrated Job's spirit, man's words piled up like yesterday's trash. To see God properly is to see ourselves correctly. One glimpse of God, and Job repented of his small view of God and distorted sense of self. But God refused to leave Job despising himself. He won't leave you there, either.

Question: How high is your view of God?

Faithlift: The higher your view of God, the higher your view of yourself.

AUGUST 2

After Job had prayed for his friends, the LORD made him prosperous again and gave him twice as much as he had before. . . . The LORD blessed the latter part of Job's life more than the first. Job 42:10, 12

Further reading: Job 40–42

God's harshest words fell on Job's comforters. To Eliphaz, God said, "I am angry with you and your two friends, because you have not spoken of me what is right, as my servant Job has. So now take seven bulls and seven rams and go to my servant Job and sacrifice a burnt offering for yourselves. My servant Job will pray for you, and I will accept his prayer and not deal with you according to your folly. You have not spoken of me what is right, as my servant Job has" (vv. 7–8). Twice God said, "You have not spoken of me what is right, as my servant Job has," underscoring the seriousness of the friend's offense. To bring about healing in their relationships with God and each other, God required sacrifices. Job's sacrifice? To pray for his persecutors. And God healed his hurting servant and prospered him like never before.

Question: Who needs the sacrifice of your prayers?

Faithlift: Obey and pray and find yourself doubly blessed and healed.

AUGUST 3

Yet when I surveyed all that my hands had done and what I had toiled to achieve, everything was meaningless, a chasing after the wind; nothing was gained under the sun. Ecclesiastes 2:11

Further reading: Ecclesiastes 1–2

King Solomon, the man who had it all, probably wrote these words. Who can't identify with feelings of futility! The writer of Ecclesiastes says what many in our culture know or suspect: there must be more to life than work and worldly success. There is.

Question: Does it encourage you to know God included honest thoughts like these in His book to you?

Faithlift: Let the One who made your hands guide their purpose.

AUGUST 4

There is a time for everything, and a season for every activity under heaven. Ecclesiastes 3:1

Further reading: Ecclesiastes 3

Is there? We have a set number of hours in each day and a

set number of days in each year. Our society's skill at accumulating clutter, cranking up blood pressure, and manufacturing choices could easily cause one to wonder whether there is truly "a time for everything and a season for every activity." But the One who inspired these words remains unshocked by our frenzied lives. And to us He would continue to underscore the timeless reality that, for all that really matters in life, *there is time.*

Question: Who is your activities coordinator?

Faithlift: Let God be your pacemaker.

August 5

Better one handful with tranquility than two handfuls with toil and chasing after the wind. Ecclesiastes 4:6

Further reading: Ecclesiastes 4

Contentment is a stranger to most of us. Like octopi we spend ourselves gathering goods, scrambling after promotions, and juggling to include one more handful. Eventually, we collapse with full hands and empty hearts. The wealthiest man, King Solomon, probably wrote, "Better one handful with tranquility. . . ." Perhaps we would do well to listen.

Question: What could you do with one free hand?

Faithlift: A content heart keeps a free hand.

August 6

Two are better than one, because they have a good return for their work. Ecclesiastes 4:9

Further reading: Ecclesiastes 4

Our culture prizes independence. Getting there on our own, making it by ourselves, and doing things our way are laudable achievements in our society. The writer of Ecclesiastes reminds us that God's best for His children includes relationships with Him and with others—interdependence and dependence. We need God and we need each other. "If one falls down, his friend can help him up. . . . Though one may be overpowered, two can defend themselves. A cord of three strands is not quickly broken" (vv. 10, 12). Our Father God loves to see us hand in hand in hand.

Question: Which way are you trying to do it?

Faithlift: Declare this day, "Dependent on God; interdependent with others."

AUGUST 7

When times are good, be happy; but when times are bad, consider: God has made the one as well as the other. Ecclesiastes 7:14

Further reading: Ecclesiastes 7

To see God only in the good times is to miss God most days.

Question: What purposes could God have in allowing bad times?

Faithlift: Look for God to make the bad times work for good.

AUGUST 8

Remember your Creator in the days of your youth, before the days of trouble come and the years approach when you will say, "I find no pleasure in them." Ecclesiastes 12:1

Further reading: Ecclesiastes 11–12

An old saying reads, "We are too soon old, and too late smart." The writer of Ecclesiastes urges us to reverse that tendency—to redeem the days while we are young and to remember God before age steals our senses. Enjoy life with God now and hereafter. Serve Him with all your heart and gifts.

Question: How old are you?

Faithlift: You are never too young or too old to redeem the time and remember your God.

AUGUST 9

The words of the wise are like goads, their collected sayings like firmly embedded nails—given by one Shepherd. Ecclesiastes 12:12

Further reading: Ecclesiastes 11–12

All wisdom finds its source in God. Some wisdom slips in quietly; other times, wise words prod us like goads. This writer calls them "firmly embedded nails." Wisdom, like a well-placed nail, stays put, demanding that we change. Our culture thrives on change yet longs for changeless truths. Whether you see God's nails as tools for puncturing your dreams or as truths for promoting your good depends on your relationship to the Shepherd.

Question: How do you view God's nails?

Faithlift: Praise God for His goads that work for our good.

AUGUST 10

Now all has been heard; here is the conclusion of the matter: Fear God and keep his commandments, for this is the whole duty of man. Ecclesiastes 12:13

Further reading: Ecclesiastes 12

Most of us suffer from information overload. The media bombards us with data, instant replays, and unwanted analyses. Our desks, bulletin boards, computers, and refrigerators spit out or show up our "to do" lists. Yet most days leave us with the nagging suspicion that we have overlooked or left undone the most important tasks. The author of Ecclesiastes simplifies his sayings and the purpose of life with one statement: "Fear God and keep his commandments, for this is the whole duty of man." Such a simple "to do" list produces more than an ordered desk or refrigerator; it produces fruits of righteousness in our lives.

Question: How does your list compare with the whole duty of man?

Faithlift: Fear God, not lists.

August 11

See! The winter is past; the rains are over and gone. Flowers appear on the earth; the season of singing has come, the cooing of doves is heard in our land. Song of Songs 2:11–12

Further reading: Song of Songs 2

To most of us who live in northern climates, spring seems to follow winter at a snail's pace. But eventually flowers peek through chilled soil and bird songs replace the scrape of snowplows. Bulky coats and boots hide in closets or attics, and screens replace storm windows and doors. Plump bodies shift from accumulating protective fat to shedding excess weight. Eventually, in the heat of August, winter may even seem like a long overdue friend. But come next January, when spring hides like buried treasure, remember Solomon's words. As sure as winter came, it will eventually leave. The same holds true for the winter of the soul. One day God will surprise you with the sight and song of spring.

Question: What season are you experiencing?

Faithlift: In the darkest winter God can surprise you with spring.

August 12

Many waters cannot quench love; rivers cannot wash it away. Song of Songs 8:7

Further reading: Song of Songs 8

This book of passionate love seems odd, wedged between the philosopher/preacher in Ecclesiastes and the prophet Isaiah. But is it? How like God to press love between the unlikely pages of a philosopher's musings and a prophet's mission! Love always belongs, whether the passionate love between a man and woman or the deep love between God and His children. Our confused world is dying for this love. God's love for us is indestructible. He expects the same between husbands and wives.

Question: How do you respond to such passionate love?

Faithlift: God will let nothing destroy His love for us.

AUGUST 13

I reared children and brought them up, but they rebelled against me. Isaiah 1:2

Further reading: Isaiah 1

This is God talking, not your next door neighbor. God, the perfect Father, has trouble with His children. There's just so much a parent can do as long as children remain free to choose.

Question: How are you using your freedom of choice?

Faithlift: Only love lets you choose.

AUGUST 14

Stop doing wrong, learn to do right! Seek justice, encourage the oppressed. Defend the cause of the fatherless, plead the case of the widow. Isaiah 1:16–17

Further reading: Isaiah 1

Wrong needs to be stopped; we must learn to do right, seek justice, encourage the oppressed and defend the fatherless and widows. As simple as it sounds, none of the above comes naturally or easily. Look at today's news.

Question: Do you know anyone who is doing everything on this list?

Faithlift: Begin to obey in one area and find encouragement and strength for the next.

AUGUST 15

Woe to those who call evil good and good evil, who put darkness for light and light for darkness, who put bitter for sweet and sweet for bitter. Woe to those who are wise in their own eyes and clever in their own sight. Isaiah 5:20–21

Further reading: Isaiah 5

These words characterize our world today. False teachers confuse and lure the unsuspecting. Don't let the packaging sell you a faulty product.

Question: Are you trusting in your wits or God's wisdom?

Faithlift: God is "good" and "light" and "sweet"—and never tricks a trusting hungry heart.

AUGUST 16

In the year that King Uzziah died, I saw the LORD seated on a throne, high and exalted, and the train of his robe filled the temple. Isaiah 6:1

Further reading: Isaiah 6

Perhaps there is no connection between the death of King Uzziah and Isaiah's unclouded vision of God. But many of us do have Uzziahs who muddy our relationship with God. Sometimes our worldly king must die before we see our heavenly king as He is and ourselves as we are.

Question: Who rules from the throne in the kingdom of your heart?

Faithlift: Keeping God on the throne of your heart is a daily discipline and delight.

AUGUST 17

"Woe to me!" I cried. "I am ruined! For I am a man of unclean lips, and I live among a people of unclean lips, and my eyes have seen the King, the Lord Almighty." Isaiah 6:5

Further reading: Isaiah 6

After Isaiah "saw the Lord seated on a throne, high and exalted," new perspective on himself and his world slapped his soul like a frigid shower on a chilly morning. To see God is to see our heart. As a prophet, Isaiah made his living through his words. Labeling himself as one with unclean lips questioned the very core of who he was and what he did. Labeling his countrymen as unclean threatened his influence on them and challenged their intention to lead a holy lifestyle. Isaiah's conclusions after confronting God: sin ruled in and around him. A glimpse of God, coupled with a long look at himself and his surroundings, left him feeling unclean and ruined. But God didn't leave him in a heap, nor will He leave us in a pile of remorse. His purpose is not to crush us but to clean us from the inside out and call us to an extraordinary, lifelong adventure with Him. Once cleansed, Isaiah heard God's call and responded as only clean folks can, "Here am I. Send me!" And God sent him on the adventure of a lifetime.

Question: Who has to put up with your lip because you've avoided a long look at God and yourself?

Faithlift: God's call is worth your complete attention.

August 18

If you do not stand firm in your faith, you will not stand at all. Isaiah 7:9

Further reading: Isaiah 7

The hearts of the king and people of Judah melted like crayons in summer sun. They were no match for the armies of Israel and Ephraim. The people trembled "as the trees of the forest are shaken by the wind" (v. 2). Then God spoke through Isaiah, "Be careful, keep calm and don't be afraid. Do not lose heart because of these two smoldering stubs of firewood" (v. 4). God reminded the king and his children that their fears were groundless. Then He challenged them, "If you do not stand firm in your faith, you will not stand at all" (v. 9). Faith is the solid ground; the rest is muck. Isaiah knew the real battle pitted faith against facts. They would need firm faith to remain standing at the end of this onslaught. And so do we.

Question: Are you committed to remain standing?

Faithlift: As we stand strong in our faith, heaven applauds.

AUGUST 19

The LORD said to me, "Take a large scroll and write on it with an ordinary pen." Isaiah 8:1

Further reading: Isaiah 8

We live in a culture that tends to assign too much power to the pen. Worshipers of the material world focus more on the instruments of their trade than on the Supplier of the message. God reminded awestruck Isaiah that the instrument was to be an ordinary pen. No need to obtain special ink, Isaiah. God demonstrated His best work against a backdrop He called ordinary, choosing ordinary pens and people to accomplish extraordinary tasks. How encouraging to note that on any ordinary day, God might do something extraordinary through your simple obedience.

Question: Are you searching for special ink when God needs your ordinary self given in full obedience?

Faithlift: God wants you, not the best tools you can buy.

AUGUST 20

Do not call conspiracy everything that these people call conspiracy; do not fear what they fear, and do not dread it. The LORD Almighty is the one you are to regard as holy, he is the one you are to fear, he is the one you are to dread. Isaiah 8:12–13

Further reading: Isaiah 8

It's easy to succumb to the concerns and fears of this world. Like nails to a magnet, we are drawn to dread the terminal instead of the eternal. God's warning to Isaiah applies to us as well. "The LORD Almighty is the one you are to regard as holy, he is the one you are to fear, he is the one you are to dread."

Question: Do you have a daily dread?

Faithlift: God will steady you if you focus on Him, not on the things you dread.

AUGUST 21

Why consult the dead on behalf of the living? Isaiah 8:19

Further reading: Isaiah 8

The practice of consulting dead counselors did not cease with the children of Israel. Our culture teems with helpless advisors—daily tips, astrology forecasts in the newspapers, and television talk shows. The less we know the living God, the more vulnerable we are to the dead weights around us.

Question: Are you vulnerable to a particularly dead form of counsel?

Faithlift: God's Word provides daily counsel for real life.

AUGUST 22

The people walking in darkness have seen a great light. Isaiah 9:2

Further reading: Isaiah 9

Imagine the sight of people bumping along, stumbling in the darkness. Picture people picking their way through life's mazes, dodging difficulties as much as possible, surrounded by never-ending night. Into such constricting misery, God shoe-horned hope. He pierced that choking despair with a pinpoint of prophetic light. Through Isaiah, God shouted to people buried in the rubble of their sins and lost dreams, "Your Messiah is coming." And like a sliver of light, hope shattered the darkness. Night knew its end.

Question: Which are you more aware of, darkness or light?

Faithlift: God saw you stumbling, too, and sent His light to shatter your darkness.

AUGUST 23

He will not judge by what he sees with his eyes, or decide by what he hears with his ears; but with righteousness he will judge the needy, with justice he will give decisions for the poor of the earth. Isaiah 11:3–4

Further reading: Isaiah 11 and Luke 1:26–38

This is bad news to a culture preoccupied with externals. With light, God again pierces dark notions about the nature of good and evil. God says to His children through Isaiah that, although the Messiah will have ears and eyes like a man, he will not behave like one. This Messiah, Jesus Christ, sees and hears with the heart of God. "The Spirit of the LORD will rest on him—the Spirit of wisdom and of understanding, the Spirit of counsel and of power, the Spirit of knowledge and of the fear of the LORD—and he will delight in the fear of the LORD" (vv. 2–3). This Messiah, too full of God to see and hear like man, comes to earth equipped with God's power and authority, shattering the world's systems and slicing through darkness with righteous light. The poor and needy will recognize with their hearts that at last they have an advocate, a Savior.

Question: Do you know someone who needs to hear this good news?

Faithlift: God is hungry for a heart-to-heart relationship with you.

AUGUST 24

You will keep in perfect peace him whose mind is steadfast, because he trusts in you. Isaiah 26:3

Further reading: Isaiah 25–26

Greeting cards, T-shirts, and bumper stickers bombard our world with external reminders of our internal lack of peace. The prophet Isaiah tells the children of Israel that one day God will settle the score with His enemies, and God's children will sing. They will sing about God's faithfulness and justice. They will sing about a perfect peace, rooted in the character of God, not in their circumstances. Their peace and song are available to you today.

Question: Do you find yourself humming?

Faithlift: The heart that trusts in God experiences perfect peace.

AUGUST 25

So then, the word of the LORD *to them will become: Do and do, do and do, rule on rule, rule on rule; a little here, a little there—so that they will go and fall backward, be injured and snared and captured. Isaiah 28:13*

Further reading: Isaiah 28

Some priests and prophets during Isaiah's day lured too many of God's children into following their systems of rules and regulations for righteous living. Systems seemed simpler than walking by faith. The seduction usually began with "a little here, a little there." There have always been unfaithful priests and prophets whose ministries have been marked by immaturity, corruption, and spiritual blindness. They badger the unwary with lists of "dos" and rules. Through Isaiah, God warns that their days and lists are numbered. To all who have refused His spiritual rest, to all who have resisted listening to Him, God's words will take a strange twist. Words like "Do and do, rule on rule, a little here, a little there" will punctuate the air and penetrate the heart with devastating consequences to the hearer. Your choices today move you forward by faith in God or backward through belief in man-made systems.

Question: Why do we tend to be vulnerable to man-made systems?

Faithlift: Faith focuses on God and moves us forward.

AUGUST 26

These people come near to me with their mouth and honor me with their lips, but their hearts are far from me. Isaiah 29:13

Further reading: Isaiah 29:1–13

Talk may be cheap, but words still impress most of us. Through words we buy, sell, instruct, persuade, flatter, tease, and soothe. Some of us approach God armed with honorable, holy sounding words. But words fall in piles and build a barricade between us and the God we seek to impress. Better to trash the words and turn to God with our whole heart.

Question: How much do you rely on words to impress God?

Faithlift: Pleasing God is a work of our hearts.

AUGUST 27

Woe to those who go to great depths to hide their plans from the LORD, who do their work in darkness and think, "Who sees us? Who will know?" Isaiah 29:15

Further reading: Isaiah 29

Secrets lurk inside most of us like buried treasure, even though their value is dubious. Some people assume their secrets are safe, since they remain convinced that God does not exist. Others are too busy covering their sins to consider the consequences. However we handle our secrets, two truths remain: nothing hides from God, and no one escapes the woe of secret sins. Trust God with your confessions and repentance. The God who sees and knows your secret sins also sees and knows your broken heart. And He forgives.

Question: Do you have any secrets?

Faithlift: Praise the God who forgives you.

Question: Can the pot say of the Potter, "He knows nothing"?

Faithlift: Tell the Potter you prefer to stay clay.

AUGUST 28

You turn things upside down, as if the potter were thought to be like the clay! Shall what is formed say to him who formed it, "He did not make me?" Can the pot say of the potter, "He knows nothing?" Isaiah 29:16

Further reading: Isaiah 29

Sound familiar? Can you identify with these Hebrew children who kept playing god? Have you ever taken a hard look at yourself and questioned if you really were made in the image of God? Have you ever felt that God knows nothing about something concerning you? Sounds like we are still turning things upside down; we are cracked pots playing at being the Potter.

AUGUST 29

In repentance and rest is your salvation, in quietness and trust is your strength, but you would have none of it. Isaiah 30:15

Further reading: Isaiah 30:1–18

Our rebellious, noisy culture contrasts starkly with God's plan for repentance and rest for His children. Then and now God grants us power to choose rebellion or repentance, rest or resistance. God gives us strength through our quiet trust in Him; unfortunately, too many of us are like the Hebrew children who "[will] have none of it." We refuse to repent, and we receive no rest.

Question: Ever wonder why there are so many tired people around?

Faithlift: Distance yourself from rebellion; discover God's rest.

AUGUST 30

Woe to those who go down to Egypt for help, who rely on horses, who trust in the multitude of their chariots and in the great strength of their horsemen, but do not look to the Holy One of Israel, or seek help from the LORD. *Isaiah 31:1*

Further reading: Isaiah 31

There will always be an "Egypt"—a place, possession, or person that represents faithless security. It's too easy to put faith in the familiar, to trust the numbers more than God's faithfulness. But "woe to those who go down to Egypt" when we were made to go up to God.

Question: Do you have an Egypt?

Faithlift: Today, call on your Father God, not your familiar god.

AUGUST 31

The grass withers and the flowers fall, but the word of our God stands forever. Isaiah 40:8

Further reading: Isaiah 40

The withered grass of August adds visual aid to this verse. God reminds His children in this chapter that they are terminal. Only God's Word stands forever. Some days it seems easier to focus on the weeds than on His Word. God help us.

Question: Where is your focus?

Faithlift: Focus on God's Word, not on the withering weeds.

SEPTEMBER

SEPTEMBER 1

He tends his flock like a shepherd: He gathers the lambs in his arms and carries them close to his heart; he gently leads those that have young. Isaiah 40:11

Further reading: Isaiah 40

This prophecy portrays Christ, the Messiah, as a tender shepherd. Sheep need a shepherd like people long for the Messiah. So God comforts His floundering flock with shepherd imagery. He tends, gathers, carries, and leads. What a relief to be a sheep when Christ is the Shepherd! Who hasn't needed to be tended, gathered, carried, or led! How many children in our world need the love of the Shepherd and long to be gathered up and hugged close to His heart! Only a stubborn donkey resists such love from the Shepherd to His sheep.

Question: Do you know a child who needs a touch from the Shepherd through you?

Faithlift: There's no greener pasture than where the Shepherd leads you.

SEPTEMBER 2

Do you not know? Have you not heard? The LORD is the everlasting God, the Creator of the ends of the earth. He will not grow tired or weary, and his understanding no one can fathom. He gives strength to the weary and increases the power of the weak. Even youths grow tired and weary, and young men stumble and fall; but those who hope in the LORD will renew their strength. They will soar on wings like eagles; they will run and not grow weary, they will walk and not be faint.
Isaiah 40:28–31

Further reading: Isaiah 40

As another summer slips into September with its packed schedules of school and work, we can benefit greatly from the message of these verses. We need God's perspective when the ordinary stresses of life sap our strength and leave us crawling when we need to run. As we come to the One who created us and our world, we read that God never tires or lacks strength. His wisdom and all His vast resources belong to His children as well. News like that gives us a running start today!

Question: "Do you not know? Have you not heard?" (Reread Isaiah 40:28–31.)

Faithlift: True fitness begins with walking with God.

SEPTEMBER 3

For I am the L*ORD, your God, who takes hold of your right hand and says to you, Do not fear; I will help you. Isaiah 41:13*

Further reading: Isaiah 41

How often God's children need to be reminded of our special relationship with Him. Our fears mount when we focus on our circumstances or limited resources for handling the problems we know we will face today. But God takes hold of our right hand and reminds us of our relationship to Him and of His limitless resources available to us. Such a God can be trusted with the knowns and unknowns of this day.

Question: Do you know a better antidote for fear?

Faithlift: Fear not: He is *your* God, holding *your* hand and helping *you* this day.

SEPTEMBER 4

But now, this is what the L*ORD says—he who created you, O Jacob, he who formed you, O Israel: "Fear not, for I have redeemed you; I have called you by name; you are mine." Isaiah 43:1*

Further reading: Isaiah 43:1–11

Can you imagine such a redemptive God calling us by name and claiming us as His own? Neither can I. But He has and He does. The unthinkable happens each day. God claims us more than we claim Him.

Question: Do others know that you belong to God?

Faithlift: Tell others of God's claim on your life.

September 5

When you pass through the waters, I will be with you; and when you pass through the rivers, they will not sweep over you. When you walk through the fire, you will not be burned; the flames will not set you ablaze. Isaiah 43:2

Further reading: Isaiah 43:1–11

All God's children go through deep waters and trials by fire. There's no if— only when. But with the *when* comes a *Who.* God never allows His children to swim alone. His buddy system is sink- and fire-proof. More sure than the *when* is the *Who.* It is God who assures His children, *"I will be with you"*—when!

Question: Can you see God in your trials by water or fire?

Faithlift: God says to you, "I will be with you whenever, wherever, and forever."

September 6

Forget the former things; do not dwell on the past. See, I am doing a new thing! Now it springs up; do you not perceive it? I am making a way in the desert and streams in the wasteland. Isaiah 43:18–19

Further reading: Isaiah 43:14–28

These words contain advice for more than just a few over-the-shoulder lookers. God's plans for His children shake up compartmentalists and confound traditionalists. Folks who hide behind secure, familiar walls may cower at God's challenge not to dwell on our past. Churches, institutions, marriages, families, and individuals sometimes limit God's "new thing." Fondly, fearfully, we clutch what we know—old behaviors and patterns that become spiritual deserts and wastelands. To all who clutch and cower God says, "Forget what was; focus on what is." And in the midst of your parched desert you will hear the sound of a babbling brook.

Question: When was the last time you heard water in your desert?

Faithlift: Forget what was; focus on what is and find water in your desert.

SEPTEMBER 7

I, even I, am he who blots out your transgressions, for my own sake, and remembers your sins no more. Isaiah 43:25

Further reading: Isaiah 43:14–28

No computer programmer or court stenographer uttered these words to people with never-ending records of wrongs. God, the Judge of all, spoke the unthinkable to the undeserving. God, who knows all, chooses to remember our sins no more. The next move is up to us.

Question: How do you respond to such mercy?

Faithlift: Thank God for choosing to remember you, not your sins.

SEPTEMBER 8

But now listen, O Jacob, my servant, Israel, whom I have chosen. This is what the LORD says—he who made you, who formed you in the womb, and who will help you: Do not be afraid, O Jacob, my servant, Jeshurun, whom I have chosen. Isaiah 44:1–2

Further reading: Isaiah 44

God spoke these words to comfort His children, reminding them of their origin and history with Him. He had chosen, made, and formed them in the womb. Now He promised help and reassurance. Life outside the womb was fraught with fears. Today, for too many, it's even more frightening inside the womb. God help us.

Question: Who would like to debate with God when life begins?

Faithlift: God chose you and will help you choose what's best this day. Don't be afraid.

SEPTEMBER 9

For I will pour water on the thirsty land, and streams on the dry ground; I will pour out my Spirit on your offspring, and my blessing on your descendants. Isaiah 44:3

Further reading: Isaiah 44

What do you desire most for your children, grandchildren, nieces, and nephews? Can you think of any greater treasure than what God has promised? What joy for grandparents, parents, aunts, and uncles to encourage the next generation to receive all God has for them and to do all God requires of them. Watch out world, when that happens!

Question: Have you considered your part in encouraging the next generation?

Faithlift: Celebrate the God who doesn't require you to sacrifice your children to Him; He sacrificed for them.

SEPTEMBER 10

I will give you the treasures of darkness, riches stored in secret places, so that you may know that I am the LORD, the God of Israel, who calls you by name. Isaiah 45:3

Further reading: Isaiah 45

Secrets hook us. Mysteries in books, on television, or in movies lure us to remain seated until we discover whodun-it, and why or how. God holds vast secrets, treasures, and riches for His children. The God who calls us by name has gifts with our names on them. But we must remain seated in His presence to discover them.

Question: Are you willing to stop running and sit down with God?

Faithlift: God has secrets and treasures with your name on them.

SEPTEMBER 11

Listen to me, O house of Jacob, all you who remain of the house of Israel, you whom I have upheld since you were conceived, and have carried since your birth. Even to your old age and gray hairs I am he, I am he who will sustain you. I have made you and I will carry you; I will sustain you and I will rescue you. Isaiah 46:3–4

Further reading: Isaiah 46

Our culture tends to devalue anything old, but especially old people. New always seems to be better. We disdain wrinkled men like wrinkled money. For birthday celebrations we prefer crisp new bills and bodies relatively free of signs of aging. To our youth-oriented culture God's words offer transfusions of hope. "Even to your old age and gray hairs . . . I will sustain you . . . I will rescue you." Thank God that He does not discard us when we grow old.

Question: How do you view growing older?

Faithlift: God puts the celebration in birthdays.

SEPTEMBER 12

This is what the LORD *says—your Redeemer, the Holy One of Israel: I am the* LORD *your God, who teaches you what is best for you, who directs you in the way you should go. Isaiah 48:17*

Further reading: Isaiah 48

Consider the personal encouragement in this verse: *Your* Redeemer, *your* God, teaches *you* what is best for *you,* and directs *you* in the way *you* should go. What does this do to whatever *you* dread most today?

Question: How teachable is your heart; how directable are your feet?

Faithlift: *Your* God has *your* best interest at heart.

SEPTEMBER 13

He made my mouth like a sharpened sword, in the shadow of his hand he hid me; he made me into a polished arrow and concealed me in his quiver. He said to me, "You are my servant, Israel, in whom I will display my splendor." But I said, "I have labored to no purpose; I have spent my strength in vain and for nothing. Yet what is due me is in the LORD*'s hand, and my reward is with my God."* Isaiah 49:2–4

Further reading: Isaiah 49:1–7

Most of us can't even count the number of times we have identified with Isaiah's sense of spent strength and squandered purpose. Endless days of diapers and dirty dishes, a call from the principal, slumping sales, being passed over for a promotion, or waiting for the next chemotherapy treatment—all contribute to a sense of helplessness and futility. Like Isaiah, we know who made us and for what purpose. But dark, exhausting days release our emotional checks; and we cry for tangible rewards, audible praise, and visible results. When nothing changes, what then? When Isaiah faced such a time, he must have wiped away the tear that escaped from his pinched eyelids and restated his faith in God. Isaiah bridged what was and what would be with one simple word: *yet.* That one word bolstered his failing confidence in himself and redirected his focus to God.

Question: Can you remember to say "yet God"?

Faithlift: The bridge between your *what was* and *what will be with God* supports you for *what is* today.

SEPTEMBER 14

I will contend with those who contend with you, and your children I will save. Isaiah 49:25

Further reading: Isaiah 49:8–26

It's easy to feel isolated, too responsible, and guilty—especially if you are a parent. Our materialistic culture demands perfection of both its products and people. But perfect we're not! So guilt, fear, and condemnation rob our joy and mar us and our loved ones. In the midst of our anguish God reminds us that we are not isolated. He desires the salvation of our children even more than we do. Children and adults need reminders that God remembers them and remains on active duty on their behalf.

Question: What do you remember about God in the middle of your problems and confusion?

Faithlift: God intends to save you and your children.

SEPTEMBER 15

The Sovereign LORD has given me an instructed tongue, to know the word that sustains the weary. He wakens me morning by morning, wakens my ear to listen like one being taught. The Sovereign LORD has opened my ears, and I have not been rebellious; I have not drawn back. Isaiah 50:4–5

Further reading: Isaiah 50

Alarm clocks and radios introduce most of us to mornings. Coffee, cereal, and commutes follow closely behind. How different our world would be if more of us were wakened by God, if we listened to His voice, and if we opened our hearts to faithful obedience. Then, whether we remained at home or headed out the door, we would be encouraged with a "word that sustains the weary," and we would be set free from our rebellious retreats to sameness.

Question: How would your world be affected?

Faithlift: Try a wakeup call from God and ask for "the word that sustains the weary."

September 16

Hear me, you who know what is right, you people who have my law in your hearts: Do not fear the reproach of men or be terrified by their insults. Isaiah 51:7

Further reading: Isaiah 51:1–16

What we hear influences what we fear. Through the prophet Isaiah, God challenged His children to listen to and fear Him, not people. We would do well to heed these words also.

Question: What do you hear? What do you fear?

Faithlift: Listening to God lessens our fears.

September 17

How beautiful on the mountains are the feet of those who bring good news, who proclaim peace, who bring good tidings, who proclaim salvation, who say to Zion, "Your God reigns!" Isaiah 52:7

Further reading: Isaiah 52:1–12

Shoe stores, shoe commercials, and shoe collections of celebrities draw our attention away from our feet to their colorful, but dispensable, coverups. Isaiah shifts our focus from what goes on our feet to where our feet must go. That's God's way. God calls "beautiful" the feet who move on up the mountain with His good news. Walking on mountains demands commitment and discipline unnecessary if we remain at the foot of the mountain. It's easy to scramble priorities and try to pretty up our feet through classy coverings instead of beautifying them through obedience to God's call.

Question: Have you seen any beautiful feet recently?

Faithlift: Carry the good news and hear God exclaim, "My, what beautiful feet you have!"

SEPTEMBER 18

He was despised and rejected by men, a man of sorrows, and familiar with suffering. Like one from whom men hide their faces he was despised, and we esteemed him not. Isaiah 53:3

Further reading: Isaiah 53

Such tender descriptions of the Messiah, the Christ of the New Testament, hang heavy on the heart. The Christ, goodness personified, met situations familiar to most of us in more limited ways. From His birth to His death on the cross He was despised and rejected, experiencing sorrow and suffering. Can we not trust such a God with our rejections and suffering? Only love would knowingly endure such undeserved suffering for our sake.

Question: How familiar are you with the One who is familiar with suffering—both His and yours?

Faithlift: Turn your face to the One who will never turn His face away from you.

SEPTEMBER 19

All your sons will be taught by the LORD, and great will be your children's peace. Isaiah 54:13

Further reading: Isaiah 54

What good news to parents, grandparents, aunts, and uncles! The Master Teacher is tenured. God will not fail to teach, or team teach with us. It's not all on our shoulders. School committees, courts, boards, nor budgets exclude God from teaching our children. Great peace results when we team up with God, the Master Teacher.

Question: Could your home use a little peace and quiet?

Faithlift: God wants to bring peace to your home.

SEPTEMBER 20

Come, all you who are thirsty, come to the waters; and you who have no money, come, buy and eat! Come, buy wine and milk without money and without cost. Isaiah 55:1

Further reading: Isaiah 55

Nothing quenches thirst like water, especially in the desert. Through Isaiah God spoke to parched souls in the desert of life, from east to west, from north and south. Lack of money can't separate anyone from living water. The only thing that can keep us from God's water is refusing to admit we're thirsty.

Question: How thirsty are you?

Faithlift: God provides living water at no cost to you in your desert today.

SEPTEMBER 21

Why spend money on what is not bread, and your labor on what does not satisfy? Listen, listen to me, and eat what is good, and your soul will delight in the richest of fare. Isaiah 55:2

Further reading: Isaiah 55

This back-to-school month also signals a return to dieting for many. God's diet plan attacks the heart of the matter. Too many of us overwork, overspend, and then overeat to simulate calm for our overstressed lives. God says, "Listen to me." That's the plan! It's a simple, two-step course. *Listen,* and then *do what He says.* God's health club starts with soul food for a healthy heart. The body will follow the dictates of the mind and heart that has decided to listen to and do God's plan.

Question: Would you like to join?

Faithlift: Shift the emphasis from thinking thin to thinking about Him.

SEPTEMBER 22

I will expose your righteousness and your works, and they will not benefit you. Isaiah 57:12

Further reading: Isaiah 57

We're into benefits in this country, even in the church. The what's-in-it-for-me virus runs largely unchecked. Our culture encourages this kind of selfish, external focus. *What we have* supposedly signifies *who we are*. How warped! In verses ten and eleven of this chapter God says to His sin-weary children, "You were wearied by all your ways, but you would not say, 'It is hopeless.' You found renewal of your strength, and so you did not faint. Whom have you so dreaded and feared that you have been false to me, and have neither remembered me nor pondered this in your hearts?" God's children caught a second wind and trekked down the wrong road, following lesser gods. The day will come for us, as it did for them, when God will expose our righteousness, our works, and it will not benefit us—unless we repent and follow God today.

Question: "Whom have you so dreaded and feared that you have been false to me, and have neither remembered me nor pondered this in your hearts?"

Faithlift: Instead of catching a second wind, ask God for a second chance.

SEPTEMBER 23

If you do away with the yoke of oppression, with the pointing finger and malicious talk, and if you spend yourselves in behalf of the hungry and satisfy the needs of the oppressed, then your light will rise in the darkness, and your night will become like the noonday. Isaiah 58:9–10

Further reading: Isaiah 58

Before claiming these promises, we must scrutinize the conditions attached to them. The spotlight requires unpopular choices. God's all-stars make tough choices under pressure. God requires us to do away with oppression, do away with the pointing finger, do away with malicious talk, then spend ourselves in behalf of the hungry and oppressed. While God's faithful few spend themselves filling such tall orders, God shines through them to lighten the darkness in a weary world.

Question: How are you spending yourself?

Faithlift: May your night become like noonday as you spend yourself for God's purposes.

SEPTEMBER 24

The LORD will guide you always; he will satisfy your needs in a sun-scorched land and will strengthen your frame. You will be like a well-watered garden, like a spring whose waters never fail. Your people will rebuild the ancient ruins and will raise up the age-old foundations; you will be called Repairer of Broken Walls, Restorer of Streets with Dwellings. Isaiah 58:11–12

Further reading: Isaiah 58

What a Father! He can't do enough for His children. He promises guidance, satisfaction of needs, strength, and purpose. God portrays His children as a lush garden, as a never-ending spring. Life in a desert terrain made this picture more prized. But look at the purpose. Do we not need today "repairers of broken walls, restorers of streets with dwellings"? Look around you and ask God to fill you with His living water, strength, and guidance so you may join His construction crew and start repairing and restoring.

Question: Where's your first construction site?

Faithlift: God's construction crew needs tender hearts, not hard hats.

SEPTEMBER 25

"If you keep your feet from breaking the Sabbath and from doing as you please on my holy day, if you call the Sabbath a delight and the LORD's holy day honorable, and if you honor it by not going your own way and not doing as you please or speaking idle words, then you will find your joy in the LORD, and I will cause you to ride on the heights of the land and to feast on the inheritance of your father Jacob."

The mouth of the LORD has spoken. Isaiah 58:13–14

Further reading: Isaiah 58

God speaks often to His children about honoring the Sabbath. In our culture we refer to Sunday as the Lord's Day. But what does it mean? One thing it does not mean is going our own way and doing as we please. Christians set in this materialistic culture must scrutinize the squeeze on our time, money, personal strength, and priorities. When every day of the week is the same, Christians target themselves as an endangered species.

Question: Does any day of the week stand out?

Faithlift: Honor God and experience new heights, joy, and His inheritance, as well.

SEPTEMBER 26

I revealed myself to those who did not ask for me; I was found by those who did not seek me. To a nation that did not call on my name, I said, "Here am I, here am I." All day long I have held out my hands to an obstinate people, who walk in ways not good, pursuing their own imaginations. Isaiah 65:1–2

Further reading: Isaiah 65

Only love perseveres through reinforced relational roadblocks. God reveals Himself; we close our eyes. God speaks; we shut our ears. God reaches with open hands; we retreat with clenched fists. No wonder we walk in ways that are not good. We continue resisting, yet God continues to woo us to Himself. Thank God for His persevering love.

Question: Have you thanked God for His persistent love?

Faithlift: Praise the God who persists, even when we turn away.

SEPTEMBER 27

This is the one I esteem: he who is humble and contrite in spirit,

and trembles at my word.
Isaiah 66:2

Further reading: Isaiah 66:1–6

The world's radically different measurements of excellence pale beside God's simple standards. Our world tends to laugh at, not laud, those who are humble and contrite. God honors those who dare to tremble at His Word. Humility and contrition are not goals for the spiritually motivated; they are a natural result of really listening to God.

Question: Whose words make you tremble?

Faithlift: Dare to really listen to God.

SEPTEMBER 28

Before I formed you in the womb I knew you, before you were born I set you apart. Jeremiah 1:5

Further reading: Jeremiah 1

Long before you knew God, God knew you. Your history, like Jeremiah's, goes back to the beginning of time. Jeremiah entered this world with a howl—and a holy call on his life. God chose Jeremiah to be His prophet, and God has a plan for your life as well. When life seems more like a baby's scream than a holy call, cry out to the God who made you. To Him you are not a second thought or a thoughtless act; you are part of His heart. You were created with purpose; your Father God knows and loves you. What a history! What a future!

Question: Have you talked over your plans with your Father God?

Faithlift: Today and tomorrow have meaning because you and God go way back.

SEPTEMBER 29

"Ah, Sovereign LORD," I said, "I do not know how to speak; I am only a child." But the LORD said to me, "Do not say, 'I am only a child.' You must go to everyone I send you to and say whatever I

command you. Do not be afraid of them, for I am with you and will rescue you," declares the L*ORD. Jeremiah 1:6–8*

Further reading: Jeremiah 1

Jeremiah was neither the first nor the last to hide behind the excuse of being too young. Like scared children we balk at each new challenge of our faith. Fear, an enemy of faith, looms like a giant, and we run and hide behind familiar skirts. We'll remain there, too, unless we turn our eyes away from the challenge and onto our Creator. Listen. God's words to Jeremiah are for you, as well. "Do not be afraid of them, for I am with you and will rescue you." This is indeed good news. God, who knows *them* as well as *you,* speaks only truth. Our God remains faithful through every generation.

Question: What does your faith say about your age?

Faithlift: Childlike faith needs no skirts to hide behind.

SEPTEMBER 30

My people have committed two sins. They have forsaken me, the spring of living water, and have dug their own cisterns, broken cisterns that cannot hold water. Jeremiah 2:13

Further reading: Jeremiah 2

Digging wells requires hard work and determination. Those who bypass God's living water for self-drilled wells do so at their own expense and sometimes at great cost to others. While society applauds doing our own thing, God knows that even our best wells can't compare with His springs of living water. What a waste when we spend our days digging when we could be drinking at God's spring!

Question: Are you tired of shoveling?

Faithlift: Stop digging; start drinking.

OCTOBER

OCTOBER 1

Stand at the crossroads and look; ask for the ancient paths, ask where the good way is, and walk in it, and you will find rest for your souls. But you said, "We will not walk in it." Jeremiah 6:16

Further reading: Jeremiah 6

This verse belongs in birthday cards for middle-aged people. Jokes about sags, wrinkles, and rusty parts leave us laughing—and longing for the fountain of youth. Certain birthdays represent crossroads. But what do we do at those junctions? God says, *stand, look, ask, walk,* and then you will *find* rest for your souls. In our fast-paced society it's a challenge to move slowly, much less stand long enough to *look, ask,* and then *walk.* It's sad that the children of Israel, would not walk in the good way. But are we really different from them? It's a daily temptation to take shortcuts to a better way. The wise person of any age will come to the crossroads and *stand, look,* and *ask.* Then, as we *walk* we will *find* what we didn't even know we needed: *rest* for our souls.

Question: Know anyone who needs a birthday boost?

Faithlift: Nothing good will pass you by while you *stand* and *seek* God.

OCTOBER 2

This is what the LORD says: "Let not the wise man boast of his wisdom or the strong man boast of his strength or the rich man boast of his riches, but let him who boasts boast about this: that he understands and knows me, that I am the LORD, who exercises kindness, justice and righteousness on earth, for in these I delight," declares the LORD. Jeremiah 9:23–24

Further reading: Jeremiah 9:12–24

Boasting seems to go naturally with wisdom, strength, and wealth. But God says, "Boast that you understand and know me." It follows that those who really know God also know better than to boast about anything else. They are too busy loving *who* God loves and doing *what* He does: showing kindness, demonstrating justice, and pressing righteousness into this earth.

Question: What are you boasting about?

Faithlift: Those who know God have something to boast about.

OCTOBER 3

Like a scarecrow in a melon patch, their idols cannot speak; they must be carried because they cannot walk. Do not fear them; they can do no harm nor can they do any good. Jeremiah 10:5

Further reading: Jeremiah 10

How like scarecrows our foolish, man-made gods appear compared to our all-knowing, all-powerful God! Such man-made concoctions should baffle only creatures who can't think. Yet God's thinking children still choose some lesser gods and fear their self-made scarecrows, who can "do no harm nor can they do any good."

Question: Does some scarecrow have you trembling?

Faithlift: Trust the God you can't carry but who chooses to carry you, as well as speak to you and walk with you.

OCTOBER 4

When your words came, I ate them; they were my joy and my heart's delight, for I bear your name, O LORD God Almighty. Jeremiah 15:16

Further reading: Jeremiah 15:11–21

While most people reject God's words, a few receive them. Jeremiah chewed on God's commandments, and they became his joy and delight. Maybe if we digested more of God's words, we'd have to swallow fewer of our own.

Question: Whose words would you rather eat?

Faithlift: A healthy diet includes a daily dose of God's words.

OCTOBER 5

But blessed is the man who trusts in the LORD, *whose confidence is in him. He will be like a tree planted by the water that sends out its roots by the stream. It does not fear when heat comes; its leaves are always green. It has no worries in a year of drought and never fails to bear fruit. Jeremiah 17:7–8*

Further reading: Jeremiah 17:5–10

God requires no green thumb to grow healthy people, only trust in God, the grower. God plants those who trust Him by a stream, not a puddle. Rooted by living water, we need not fear heat or drought. God will produce new growth and fruit in our lives. What a healthy, purposeful life cycle.

Question: Are you hoping for a green thumb, or are you trusting the Grower to produce fruit in your life?

Faithlift: Thumbs down to anything less than trust in God.

OCTOBER 6

"For I know the plans I have for you," declares the LORD, *"plans to prosper you and not to harm you, plans to give you hope and a future. Then you will call upon me and come and pray to me, and I will listen to you. You will seek me and find me when you seek me with all your heart." Jeremiah 29:11–13*

Further reading: Jeremiah 29:4–14

Most children love to play hide and seek. No one wants to be found immediately, but neither do they want to remain hidden and forgotten. God promises to be visible to all whole-hearted seekers. God doesn't play games with us, even seemingly harmless ones like hide and seek. And for all who find Him, it's an eternal case of finder's keepers.

Question: Are you trying to play games with God?

Faithlift: God places Himself in the open for all whole-hearted seekers and presents His much-sought-after children with everlasting love and long-range plans.

OCTOBER 7

Call to me and I will answer you and tell you great and unsearchable things you do not know. Jeremiah 33:3

Further reading: Jeremiah 33

Imprisoned Jeremiah received hopeful words from his God about his future and the future of God's children. Our all-powerful, all-knowing God longs for communication with His children. Like a parent to a child away at camp or college for the first time, God says, "Call home." And for those who call and listen, He "will answer you and tell you . . . great and unsearchable things."

Question: Do you need a nudge to call home?

Faithlift: Your Father God is always home when you call.

OCTOBER 8

Ebed-Melech the Cushite said to Jeremiah, "Put these old rags and worn-out clothes under your arms to pad the ropes." Jeremiah did so. Jeremiah 38:12

Further reading: Jeremiah 38:1–13

What a story! King Zedekiah was a wimp. Weary of the warnings God kept posting through His prophet, he turned God's man Jeremiah over to some disgruntled officials. They took Jeremiah from his imprisonment in the courtyard of the guard and "lowered Jeremiah by ropes into the cistern; it had no water in it, only mud, and Jeremiah sank down into the mud" (v. 6). Such cruel punishment for one of God's faithful few! Old Jeremiah could have wasted away in that well, but God, his maker and manager, enlisted support from Ebed-Melech, an official in the king's palace. After hearing of Jeremiah's plight from Ebed-Melech, King Zedekiah commanded the godly official to choose thirty men to "lift Jeremiah the prophet out of the cistern before he die[d]" (v. 10). But God's servant Ebed went beyond the call of duty. He gathered old rags and worn-out clothes from the basement of the palace, then lowered them down to Jeremiah. Ebed-Melech, cushioned the ropes for Jeremiah's frail old arms. We could use some men and women today who go beyond duty and cushion the ropes.

Question: Who needs your cushion of support today?

Faithlift: God loves when you go beyond the call of duty and cushion the ropes.

OCTOBER 9

He has walled me in so I cannot escape; he has weighed me down with chains. Even when I call out or cry for help, he shuts out my prayer. He has barred my way with blocks of stone; he has made my paths crooked.
Lamentations 3:7–9

Further reading: Lamentations 3

Jeremiah was a failure. He had spent his life prophesying punishment for God's disobedient children, warning of destruction to come. All his warnings went unheeded. Instead of being lauded for speaking God's truth, he was laughed at, ignored, and punished. But when judgment hit,

Jeremiah didn't laugh and get even; he lamented. Broken Jeremiah bowed under the weight of disappointment and seeming defeat. His cries to God hit low ceilings and crashed down on his despairing soul. Daily dialogues with God turned to mumbled monologues. God's creative plan for his life looked more like crooked paths. Does God have a word of encouragement in the middle of this maze of despair? Yes! Success with God is measured by faithfulness. Jeremiah had remained faithful; he was not a failure in God's eyes. Only disobedient and ignorant people labeled him a loser. We can derive encouragement from the fact that God let us know of Jeremiah's defeats and despair. When we're hiding in defeat, we can recall one of God's faithful few who felt alone and unheard, yet remained faithful.

Question: Can you identify with Jeremiah?

Faithlift: Success with God is called: faithful.

OCTOBER 10

I remember my affliction and my wandering, the bitterness and the gall. I well remember them, and my soul is downcast within me. Yet this I call to mind and therefore I have hope.
Lamentations 3:19–21

Further reading: Lamentations 3

What would we do without the word *yet!* Remembering afflictions comes too easily, especially when we are tired, sick, or discouraged. Our remembrances come naturally, but to say "yet" requires supernatural strength and a will to remember God's faithfulness. Despair comes from remembering our trials without hoping in the God who calls us to say, "Yet will I trust in Him." Jeremiah found hope when he remembered the Lord's great love and His unfailing compassions (see v. 22). Faith chooses to say "yet" and finds hope in one small word.

Question: What do you do when you lack hope?

Faithlift: Faith chooses to say "yet" and finds hope in the process.

OCTOBER 11

Because of the LORD's great love we are not consumed, for his compassions never fail. They are new every morning; great is your faithfulness. I say to myself, "The LORD is my portion: therefore I will wait for him."
Lamentations 3:22–24

Further reading: Lamentations 3

Better than fresh bread is fresh compassion, "new every morning." We all know reasons why we do not deserve even the smallest amount of God's loving compassion. But to find fresh compassion on the doorstep of our hearts each morning is unthinkable. Jeremiah was left talking to himself, not as a deranged prophet, but as an awed child, plate piled high with his favorite food, and seated beside his faithful friend.

Question: What do you say to yourself about your God?

Faithlift: Great is God's faithfulness to you each day.

OCTOBER 12

I will give them an undivided heart and put a new spirit in them; I will remove from them their heart of stone and give them a heart of flesh. Then they will follow my decrees and be careful to keep my laws. They will be my people, and I will be their God.
Ezekiel 11:19–20

Further reading: Ezekiel 11:16–25 and 36:26–28

An undivided heart requires a spiritual heart transplant. God is ready when you are.

Question: When was your last heart checkup?

Faithlift: God's patients always live.

OCTOBER 13

Now this was the sin of your sister Sodom: She and her daughters were arrogant, overfed and unconcerned; they did not help the poor and needy. Ezekiel 16:49

Further reading: Ezekiel 16

God takes seriously the plight of the poor and needy. We who claim to be His children need to check our fascination with the good life and our claims to prosperity and blessing at the expense of some of our brothers and sisters. Only the arrogant and unconcerned stuff themselves and starve their neighbors.

Question: What do you have to share?

Faithlift: God's children love to share.

OCTOBER 14

I looked for a man among them who would build up the wall and stand before me in the gap on behalf of the land so I would not have to destroy it, but I found none. Ezekiel 22:30

Further reading: Ezekiel 22

Moses stood in the breach when God determined to destroy the complaining Israelites (see Psalm 106:23), and Abraham pleaded with God to spare Sodom (see Genesis 18). Sometimes God finds a faithful man, woman, boy, or girl to stand in the gap. There has never been a time when faithful folk were obsolete, even today. God is still looking for faithful childen.

Question: Are your hands in your pockets or in the air?

Faithlift: Faith stands in the gap between God and man.

OCTOBER 15

So I prophesied as he commanded me, and breath entered them; they came to life and stood up on their feet—a vast army. Ezekiel 37:10

Further reading: Ezekiel 37:1–14

Ezekiel, knee-deep in a valley of bones, stared when God interrupted with a question: "Son of man, can these bones live?" (v. 3)

Ezekiel must have scratched his old head, then thought better of his gut response. "O Sovereign LORD, you alone know" (v. 3). Ezekiel spoke the truth. God did know. God breathed life into the piles of bones, which rattled and responded to their Creator's commands. God pulled down the screen and previewed a movie for Ezekiel—a picture of God's spiritually dried up children. The children of Israel lamented, "Our bones are dried up and our hope is gone; we are cut off" (v. 11). But God heard their cry and commanded Ezekiel to proclaim, "This is what the Sovereign LORD says: 'O my people, I am going to open your graves and bring you up from them; I will bring you back to the land of Israel. Then you, my people, will know that I am the LORD, when I open your graves and bring you up from them. I will put my Spirit in you and you will live'" (vv. 12–14). Those bones didn't just rattle around. They "stood up on their feet—a vast army." That same Spirit breathes life today into fresh recruits. Praise the God who sees potential in a bag of bones!

Question: Do you believe God can energize your spiritually tired bones?

Faithlift: Praise the God who resurrects what others reject.

OCTOBER 16

They [the priests] are to teach my people the difference between the holy and the common and show them how to distinguish between the unclean and the clean.
Ezekiel 44:23

Further reading: Ezekiel 44

Responsible leaders, teachers, preachers, rabbis, and parents use the show-and-tell technique. Telling alone deprives the learner of the teacher's prime tool for relaying truth: example. God instructed the priests to *teach* the difference and to *show* how to distinguish. Too many of us erroneously believe that "show and tell" belongs in kindergarten.

In fact, we never outgrow our need to see and hear, or our responsibility to show and tell others the good news.

Question: Who has been a strong example for you?

Faithlift: God's children who *show* the difference *make* a difference.

OCTOBER 17

But Daniel resolved not to defile himself. Daniel 1:8

Further reading: Daniel 1

Captivity revealed true character in Daniel and a few of his young Hebrew friends. Scripture does not mention the parents of these young men, but one wonders what course of action they took while their sons adjusted to another way of life. Did they fret, curse, fear, or plot the government's overthrow? Our best clues come from their children. Away from familiar people and parameters, Daniel "purposed in his heart." You don't learn purpose in the king's court; you catch it as a kid from the people around you. Daniel's parents, wherever they were, probably resisted natural tendencies to bind themselves and their son with fear. It is much more likely that they prayed and linked each other with God, whose power was more than enough to give their boy Daniel some extra resolve.

Question: What do you learn about yourself when you're far away from familiar people and parameters?

Faithlift: Prayer fortifies the purpose of your heart to obey God.

OCTOBER 18

Shadrach, Meshach and Abednego replied to the king, "O Nebuchadnezzar, we do not need to defend ourselves before you in this matter. If we are thrown into the blazing furnace, the God we serve is able to save us from it, and he will rescue us from your hand, O king. But even if he does not, we want you to know, O king, that we will not serve your gods or worship the image of gold you have set up." Daniel 3:16–18

Further reading: Daniel 3

Like Daniel, these young Hebrew men had settled their hearts and minds long before they stood before an irate king. Confident in their God, these young men confronted their king and fed the fire of his rage with their resolve. Most of us could handle phase one, the part where we challenge God to a duel with our enemy. It's part two where we're apt to slink away, beg for mercy, or request time to rethink our position. We choke on the "but even if [God] does not [intervene]." These young men, however, never broke stride. Their unflappable faith left Nebuchadnezzar ranting, raving, and revving up the furnace. The king commanded his servants to bind up these boys and toss them into a fire so intense it destroyed the king's servants. But God heard his boys praising His name, not pleading for mercy. No way was God going to let them become ashes in the eyes of these blaspheming Babylonians! The presence of Almighty God brought these young men through the fire with their faith in God unsinged. And a courtful of new converts welcomed them.

Question: How do you view God when the heat's on?

Faithlift: Faith grows best under fire.

OCTOBER 19

So Shadrach, Meshach and Abednego came out of the fire, and the satraps, prefects, governors and royal advisers crowded around them. They saw that the fire had not harmed their bodies, nor was a hair of their heads singed; their robes were not scorched, and there was no smell of fire on them. Daniel 3:26–27

Further reading: Daniel 3

In Daniel 1:6–7 we learn that the Babylonians renamed these young Judean men. Erasing their Hebrew names, however, stole nothing from their faith in God. These young captives looked so good and served so well that promotions, not punishments, were their lot—that is, until word came that they refused to bow to Nebuchadnezzar's gods and golden image. Their testimony to God's greatness and faithfulness did not spare them from a trial by fire. But in the middle of it, God remained with them; and they stepped out unsinged. The court officials and advisers inched closer, sniffing and staring. Unbelievable! No singed hair, no scorched robes, no smell of fire! No other alternative remained to Nebuchadnezzar but to praise the God of Shadrach, Meshach, and Abednego and to give them a promotion.

Question: How do you smell when you step from the fire?

Faithlift: Faith under fire leaves no singe, scorch, or smell.

OCTOBER 20

Three times a day [Daniel] got down on his knees and prayed, giving thanks to his God, just as he had done before. Daniel 6:10

Further reading: Daniel 6:1–12

"Now Daniel so distinguished himself among the administrators and the satraps by his exceptional qualities that the king planned to set him over the whole kingdom" (v. 3). Some envious men tried to muddy his reputation, "but they were unable to do so. They could find no corruption in him, because he was trustworthy and neither corrupt nor negligent" (v. 4). So they played on the king's vanity and lured him to issue the following decree: "Anyone who prays to any god or man during the next thirty days, except to you, O king, shall be thrown into the lions' den" (v. 7). When Daniel learned of the decree, he neither cowered nor capitulated; he simply continued his usual practice and prayed. We desperately need some daring Daniels today whose usual practice is prayer.

Question: Do you dare to be a Daniel?

Faithlift: More time on your knees gives less time to your critics.

October 21

The king said to Daniel, "May your God, whom you serve continually, rescue you!" Daniel 6:16

Further reading: Daniel 6:11–28

The decree snared the king as well as Daniel and left King Darius desperate to save Daniel, his distinguished leader, from the consequences of disobeying his anti-prayer legislation (see vv. 1–14). But the sun set before the king found a legal loophole, and Daniel was dumped into the lions' den. King Darius probed every angle humanly possible to spare Daniel, until in desperate hope he cried to Daniel, "May your God, whom you serve continually, rescue you." No one served the king better than Daniel; yet the king recognized Daniel's God as the power behind Daniel's skills and distinguished service. Consequently, this despairing king hoped desperately that Daniel's devotion to God would not go unnoticed. It didn't!

Question: How does your service to others reflect your devotion to God?

Faithlift: Devotion to God shows on the job.

October 22

At the first light of dawn, the king got up and hurried to the lions' den. When he came near the den, he called to Daniel in an anguished voice, "Daniel, servant of the living God, has your God, whom you serve continually, been able to rescue you from the lions?" Daniel answered, " . . . They have not hurt me. . . ." The king was overjoyed and gave orders to lift Daniel out of the den. And when Daniel was lifted from the den, no wound was found on him, because he had trusted in his God. Daniel 6:19–23

Further reading: Daniel 6

Anguished onlookers, curious critics, and sober seekers throughout history race the dawn, like King Darius, to see if God's Daniels have survived their lions' dens. Some, like Daniel, have lived to praise God in the morning, while others who loved and trusted God just as much have become a lion's lunch or worse. The mystery remains: God, always able to rescue His children from lions' dens, sometimes allows His choicest children to remain. As a result, some of the witnesses turn quickly to follow the God who rescues His children. At other times, men, women, or children deliberately choose to give their lives to the God of martyrs, a God who allowed some to remain.

Question: Where is God when there is no rescue?

Faithlift: May your faith and trust in God, in or out of the den, point the onlookers, critics, and seekers to trust your God.

OCTOBER 23

[Daniel prayed to the Lord and confessed:] "O Lord, the great and awesome God, who keeps his covenant of love with all who love him and obey his commands, we have sinned and done wrong. We have been wicked and have rebelled; we have turned away from your commands and laws. We have not listened to your servants the prophets. . . . Lord, you are righteous, but this day we are covered with shame." Daniel 9:4–7.

Further reading: Daniel 9

Daniel's use of *we* in his prayer probes our hearts and prompts us to consider our tendencies to trivialize prayer and distance ourselves from the sins of others. Daniel's slate seemed clean. Why mess it up with the sins of others? Daniel's prayer demonstrated a deep knowledge of God. The more we know God, the more we identify with His suffering and sinful children. Daniel, part of God's family, suffered the consequences of human sin and sought God's mercy for His children. Personal peace and prosperity didn't entice Daniel to distance himself from the pain of others. Like his God, Daniel so loved his world that he involved himself through prayer and participation in it.

Question: Why bother to pray for everyone?

Faithlift: God loves and responds to our corporate prayers and actions.

OCTOBER 24

Then he continued, "Do not be afraid, Daniel. Since the first day that you set your mind to gain understanding and to humble yourself before your God, your words were heard, and I have come in response to them. But the prince of the Persian kingdom resisted me twenty-one days." Daniel 10:12–13

Further reading: Daniel 10

Daniel, famished and fatigued from fasting and praying, stood on a river bank. A divine messenger brought him reassuring words. "Do not be afraid. . . . Your words were heard . . . I have come in response to them." Most of us never receive a vision or host a divine messenger; nor do most of us mourn and fast for three weeks. Daniel did both. It must have been harder for Daniel to wait for the answer than to do without the food for twenty-one days. Both fasting and waiting tax us in our age of instant gratification. We're too focused on doing with, to choose to do without, even for a day. That may explain why there are so few Daniels.

Question: How well do you wait?

Faithlift: Learn to wait.

OCTOBER 25

The LORD said to me, "Go, show your love to your wife again, though she is loved by another and is an adulteress. Love her as the LORD loves the Israelites, though they turn to other gods and love the sacred raisin-cakes." Hosea 3:1

Further reading: Hosea 3

God's toughest assignment to the best of men and women is to love one who loves another. No one knows better than God the pain of rejection, the sacrifice of reaching out in love to a recoiling lover.

Question: How has God demonstrated His love to you in the past twenty-four hours?

Faithlift: Dare to love again, for God's sake.

OCTOBER 26

The Israelites are stubborn, like a stubborn heifer. How then can the LORD pasture them like lambs in a meadow? Hosea 4:16

Further reading: Hosea 4

The metaphor of sheep and shepherds runs through the Old and New Testaments. Sheep simply follow their leader. Heifers, like donkeys, know a better way. The Shepherd leads the sheep to green pastures, quiet streams, prepared tables and more (see Psalm 23). Heifers and donkeys, which habitually stray beyond their fences, may overeat and bloat or taste the unkindnesses of a new owner. As near as a heart's choice, however, the Lord of lambs waits for any who choose to follow His lead.

Question: How would the Shepherd describe you?

Faithlift: The grass is always greener by the Shepherd's side.

OCTOBER 27

Foreigners sap his strength, but he does not realize it. His hair is sprinkled with gray, but he does not notice. Hosea 7:9

Further reading: Hosea 7

Self-deception ages us spiritually. Growing older differs from maturing. The children of Israel aged prematurely because they were unwilling to separate themselves from the practices of their heathen neighbors. Unlike Daniel, who "resolved not to defile himself" (Daniel 1:8), too many of

God's children deluded themselves that "a little of this or that" would make no difference. But bit by bit they became rebellious, like those around them, instead of restored, as God had planned. Most of us will grow old, lose strength, and find gray hair an unavoidable part of the aging process. But to age—not mature—through spiritual deterioration is avoidable. We need only obey and stop deceiving ourselves.

Question: How are you combating spiritual aging?

Faithlift: Obedience keeps you young at heart.

OCTOBER 28

Sow for yourselves righteousness, reap the fruit of unfailing love, and break up your unplowed ground; for it is time to seek the LORD, *until he comes and showers righteousness on you.*
Hosea 10:12

Further reading: Hosea 10

If Israel needed this reminder of their purpose and God's provision, how much more do we need to heed these words. Like Israel, we busy ourselves sowing. But what are we sowing? The law of the harvest states that whatever you sow, you reap. Israel "planted wickedness" and "reaped evil" (v. 13). What have we planted, and what are we reaping? The time is long overdue for us to "break up [our] unplowed ground," to sow "righteousness," and to "seek the LORD."

Question: What are you sowing?

Faithlift: It's not too late to sow righteousness.

OCTOBER 29

When Israel was a child, I loved him . . . It was I who taught Ephraim to walk, taking them by the arms; but they did not realize it was I who healed them. I led them with cords of human kindness, with ties of love; I lifted the yoke from their neck and bent down to feed them. Hosea 11:1, 3–4

Further reading: Hosea 11

What a tender picture of God the Father, looking lovingly upon His children, teaching, leading, healing, lifting, and feeding them. Sadly, some of God's children never grow up to realize who their Father is or how much He loves them. God is still loving, teaching, leading, healing, lifting, and feeding. Are we any better at recognizing Him than the children of Israel were?

Question: Does God have your attention?

Faithlift: Thank God for being such a great Father.

OCTOBER 30

But I am the LORD *your God, who brought you out of Egypt. You shall acknowledge no God but me, no Savior except me. I cared for you in the desert, in the land of burning heat. When I fed them, they were satisfied; when they were satisfied, they became proud; then they forgot me.* Hosea 13:4–6

Further reading: Hosea 13

The marks of ungratefulness—fed, satisfied, proud, and forgetful—characterize God's immature children. We slap our foreheads, cluck our tongues at these Israelite ingrates, then miss the manna on our tables. God gets our attention in times of despair but loses many of us in times of prosperity. We turn our focus to material possessions and forget our Savior. And history repeats itself at our expense.

Question: What does your life illustrate about your focus?

Faithlift: Thank God today for filling your life with His loving kindness.

OCTOBER 31

Take words with you and return to the LORD. *Say to him: "Forgive all our sins and receive us graciously, that we may offer the fruit of our lips."* Hosea 14:2

Further reading: Hosea 14

We live in a highly mobile society. Jobs and interests require frequent travel or relocation. Airport terminals house stores and shops for traveling shoppers who need a little something to bring back to the kids, spouse, boss, or friend. What about the gift of words? "Take words with you." Are there children, spouses, friends, or colleagues who could benefit more from a "forgive me, please" than from fresh flowers or fascinating toys?

Question: Could your relationship with God or someone else use the gift of words?

Faithlift: Repent, return to the Lord, then head home and "take words with you."

NOVEMBER

NOVEMBER 1

Tell it to your children, and let your children tell it to their children, and their children to the next generation. Joel 1:3

Further reading: Joel 1

Our children need more than encouraging words and positive pats. Add straight teeth, private lessons, compact discs, videos, fashionable clothes, and they'll still come up empty. We spend our energy for straight teeth and stereos and find no reserves for training children to walk the straight and narrow. God's demands are telling. Our children need to see in us and hear from us their history—not only United States and world history, but God's history with His children and our family history with God. We remind and nag about napkins, elbows, toothbrushes, and dirty boots but forget to tell God's views of sin, stewardship of earth and other resources, standards for real life, and of His faithfulness to all generations. What are we saying about a holy God when we devote more attention to elbows than to eternal issues?

Question: How telling are your gifts to your children?

Faithlift: Keep telling the story the next generation is dying to hear.

NOVEMBER 2

"Even now," declares the LORD, "return to me with all your heart, with fasting and weeping and mourning." Rend your heart and not your garments. Return to the LORD your God, for he is gracious and compassionate, slow to anger and abounding in love. Joel 2:12–13

Further reading: Joel 2

God's patience, compassion, and gracious heart reach to all readers and hearers of this good news. With our backlog of sins and history of rebellion we blink and shake our weary heads at the possibility of another chance. But God, "slow to anger and abounding in love," reaches out with open arms and an open invitation: "even now, return to me with all your heart."

Question: What keeps you from returning?

Faithlift: Your open heart to God's invitations will open a whole new world for you.

NOVEMBER 3

And afterward, I will pour out my Spirit on all people. Your sons and daughters will prophesy, your old men will dream dreams, your young men will see visions. Even on my servants, both men and women, I will pour out my Spirit in those days.
Joel 2:28–29

Further reading: Joel 2

How encouraging this verse is to women who doubt their place in God's plan! How affirming to all who feel too young or too old for God to use! How like God to shake up man-made categories!

Question: Are you encouraged?

Faithlift: Praise the God who breaks open our cages and bids us to fly.

NOVEMBER 4

The words of Amos, one of the shepherds of Tekoa. . . . Amos 1:1

Further reading: Amos 1

"Strange verse to select," some may say. "Doesn't grab me," say others. But look closer. A simple shepherd authored this book. God selected a shepherd! No theologian, priest, rabbi, or distinguished leader lifted the quill to pen this scroll! A simple shepherd! What kind of a God picks a social outcast like a shepherd to do His bidding! The kind of

God you and I desperately need.

Question: What encouragement do you find in God's love and purpose for one simple shepherd?

Faithlift: Praise the God of shepherds and sinners like you and me.

NOVEMBER 5

This is what the L*ORD says: "For three sins of Israel, even for four, I will not turn back my wrath. They sell the righteous for silver, and the needy for a pair of sandals." Amos 2:6*

Further reading: Amos 2

Our generous God hates greed! When we trample some*one* for some*thing,* we set ourselves up for God's judgment. If getting ahead involves trampling someone else, we'd better get off that ladder. The more we know the needy, the more naturally we will respond to sharing our sandals instead of selling souls.

Question: Do you know any truly needy person by name?

Faithlift: The greater our love for God, the greater our love for all His children.

NOVEMBER 6

But you made the Nazirites drink wine and commanded the prophets not to prophesy. Amos 2:12

Further reading: Amos 2

The Nazirites stood out by what they did and how they looked. Like Samson in the book of Judges, Nazirites were known for long hair and beards and as non-drinkers of wine. Nazirites did this, not as social commentary, but in obedience to the God they loved. Today, maybe more so than during Samson's days, we muddy God's mandate for holy living by our casual commitments and inconsistent convictions. Unintentionally, we slip a drink to a "Nazirite" and silence prophetic words.

Many in today's society view intolerance as the greatest sin. In that kind of environment, nobody wants to stand out as a Nazirite or divide by a prophetic word. Alcoholic abstinence is not the issue; obedience to God's call and support for those who follow God's different but definite call is. Sometimes those who commit to follow God at any cost pay most dearly among their brothers and sisters in the faith, who make them sip wine and silence their prophets so they won't stand out and embarrass them.

Question: How encouraging are you to those who commit to follow God at a different cost from yours?

Faithlift: Mature brothers and sisters keep the focus on faithfully standing up for God's standards, not on fearfully standing out from the surrounding culture.

NOVEMBER 7

Seek good, not evil, that you may live. Then the LORD *God Almighty will be with you, just as you say he is. Amos 5:14*

Further reading: Amos 5

Most of us find what we seek. God commands us to "seek good . . . that [we] may live." What we seek reveals what we really believe. Throughout the Old Testament we read stories of those who seek only their own good. God grants real life and the pleasure of His company to all who do the difficult daily task of seeking good.

Question: What are you seeking and how does it show?

Faithlift: Seek good and find God in this day.

NOVEMBER 8

I hate, I despise your religious feasts; I cannot stand your assemblies. Even though you bring me burnt offerings and grain offerings, I will not accept them. Though you bring choice fellowship offerings, I will have no regard for them. Amos 5:21–22

Further reading: Amos 5

God is more than unimpressed by our religious words, and He despises meaningless rituals designed to impress onlookers. How much of what we do today would God despise or find unacceptable? Most of us are too busy doing what we think is the right thing, to stop and ask questions of God and ourselves. God isn't picky and hard to please; we're just trying to look good without being good.

Question: What questions do you need to be asking?

Faithlift: God is pleased when we work wholeheartedly, for His eyes only.

NOVEMBER 9

Away with the noise of your songs! I will not listen to the music of your harps. But let justice roll on like a river, righteousness like a never-failing stream! Amos 5:23–24

Further reading: Amos 5

These verses sound as though God is more interested in our courts than our choirs, in our prison ministries than in our praise services. The truth is that God wants both. But are we so busy rehearsing or hunting soloists for our Sunday services that we cannot hear the hurting souls who cry for justice? God isn't. It's easier to make a religious noise than to right a wrong. God loves the sound of justice being practiced.

Question: Can those who cry for justice count on you?

Faithlift: Make the joyful noise of justice.

NOVEMBER 10

"The days are coming," declares the Sovereign LORD, "when I will send a famine through the land—not a famine of food or a thirst for water, but a famine of hearing the words of the LORD." Amos 8:11

Further reading: Amos 8

We live in a world of words, both written and spoken. Television, radio, and newspapers bombard us with the latest word on world and local happenings. Tapes motivate our jogging and inform or soothe our commutes. Surrounded by the best of man-made words, do we miss God's?

Question: Which words do you live and die by?

Faithlift: Feast on God's words today.

NOVEMBER 11

You should not look down on your brother in the day of his misfortune. Obadiah 1:12

Further reading: Obadiah 1

Television invites us daily to view the misfortunes of our brothers and sisters at home and around the world. It's simplistic, arrogant, and un-Biblical to look down on them and feel smugly secure. If we resist loving the world and insist on looking down on our unfortunate brothers and sisters, we do so at our personal and national peril.

Question: How do you respond to misfortunes beyond your small world?

Faithlift: As God's child, resist the natural tendency to look down instead of up.

NOVEMBER 12

The day of the LORD is near for all nations. As you have done, it will be done to you; your deeds will return upon your own head. Obadiah 1:15

Further reading: Obadiah 1

Most of us grew up hearing the golden rule: "Do unto others as you would have them do unto you." God pushes His children beyond their personal back yards to a global golden rule. Linked by satellites, computers, television, and jet travel, we know of worlds beyond our small one. But with knowledge comes responsibility. Personal, national, and global costs skyrocket when we knowingly do wrong or purposely withhold our help. To obey God's global golden rule is to love as God loves. Giving God's love never harms the giver or the recipient.

Question: How global are your concerns?

Faithlift: You make a world of difference as you obey God's global golden rule.

NOVEMBER 13

The word of the LORD came to Jonah son of Amittai: "Go to the great city of Nineveh and preach against it, because its wickedness has come up before me." But Jonah ran away from the LORD and headed for Tarshish. He went down to Joppa, where he found a ship bound for that port.
Jonah 1:1–3

Further reading: Jonah 1

Did you ever run away from one of God's assignments? You probably didn't go "down to Joppa," but it was *down* to somewhere or with someone. When running away from God seems as easy as a downhill slide, remember Jonah, and move up to God's challenge instead of down in disobedience.

Question: Can you identify with Jonah? How?

Faithlift: Faith accepts the challenge.

NOVEMBER 14

Then the LORD sent a great wind on the sea, and such a violent storm arose that the ship threatened to break up . . . but Jonah had gone below deck, where he lay down and fell into a deep sleep. The captain went to him and said, "How can you sleep? Get up and call on your god! Maybe he will take notice of us, and we will not perish."
Jonah 1:4–6

Further reading: Jonah 1

Deep sleep and peace of mind and heart are not always synonymous. Sometimes we sleep to forget or to delay the inevitable. It's called the sleep of avoidance. We crave sleep when that paper needs writing or a book needs reading. When the lawn needs mowing, a nap looks good. We think a quick snooze will clear our minds to grade that stack of papers. Or we catch a few winks before we tackle the basement. Most of the time, we hurt more than ourselves when we try to sleep things off. While Jonah slept, the captain and his crew feared going down with their ship. Finally, the captain shook Jonah and said, "How can you sleep? Get up and call on your god!"—a good question followed by good advice!

Question: Have you ever tried to solve something with a Jonah-like nap?

Faithlift: Get up and call on your God; He never sleeps.

NOVEMBER 15

"Pick me up and throw me into the sea", he replied, "and it will become calm. I know that it is my fault that this great storm has come upon you." Instead, the men did their best to row back to land. Jonah 1:12–13

Further reading: Jonah 1

Courage and cowardice dwell within each of us. Jonah, unwilling and afraid, refused to preach to the Ninevites. He fled to the bottom of a ship and took a coward's nap until the captain and his crew interrupted his sleep. Without pretending, passing the buck, or placating the crew until he saw a safe alternative to shore, Jonah simply said, "Pick me up and throw me into the sea." How foolish his solution would seem to men who feared the sea and death by drowning! The crew had a different solution: row! But Jonah won out, because the rowers only knew the sea, while Jonah knew the God who made the sea.

Question: Have you ever had an *instead* for one of God's plans for you?

Faithlift: When you know the God who made the land and sea, it's easier to trust Him in any circumstance.

NOVEMBER 16

From inside the fish Jonah prayed to the LORD *his God. Jonah 2:1*

Further reading: Jonah 2

Modern technology tracks the sounds of whales as they glide through deep waters. God recorded Jonah's prayer inside a whale's belly without sonar. Why? God knew how often His children would find themselves in deep water. He knew Jonah would not be the last to have a better plan for his life than God's. And God must have wanted one fish story to be about a man who got away, but only for awhile.

Question: What does it do for you to know that God is tracking your sound?

Faithlift: God is tuned in to your faintest cry on land or sea.

NOVEMBER 17

When my life was ebbing away, I remembered you, LORD, *and my prayer rose to you, to your holy temple. Jonah 2:7*

Further reading: Jonah 2

Jonah, whipped by currents and tangled in seaweed, sank to the ocean's floor, "to the roots of the mountains" (v. 6). While captain and crew enjoyed calm seas and offered sacrifices to Jonah's awesome God (see 1:16), Jonah fought his watery prison and cried to his God. And from the deep waters a strong, silent friend slipped up and slurped down Jonah. For three days and nights this friendly fish housed a penitent preacher. What do you do in the belly of a whale? You don't play games. Jonah stopped playing and remembered the Lord. And he slowly realized that God had never forgotten him.

Question: When are you most apt to remember the Lord?

Faithlift: You can't sink below God's reach.

NOVEMBER 18

Those who cling to worthless idols forfeit the grace that could be theirs. Jonah 2:8

Further reading: Jonah 2

Jonah groped around this large-bellied aquarium and found nothing familiar about his floating home, save the smell of fish. With nothing but time and water on his hands, Jonah reflected. Isolated from the trappings of a lifetime, Jonah must have realized he had amassed quite a collection of idols. He wasn't just talking about others when he exclaimed, "Those who cling to worthless idols forfeit the grace that could be theirs." He had fled from grace when he refused to preach in Nineveh. Yet, despite Jonah's disobedience, God reached in love to reel in his rebellious preacher. Instead of drowning, Jonah experienced God's grace.

Question: What does it mean to forfeit the grace that could be yours?

Faithlift: Look for God's grace in your life today.

NOVEMBER 19

"But I, with a song of thanksgiving, will sacrifice to you. What I have vowed I will make good. Salvation comes from the LORD." And the LORD commanded the fish, and it vomited Jonah onto dry land. Jonah 2:9–10

Further reading: Jonah 2

Jonah, out of man's sight but not God's, assessed the circumstances behind his unwanted dive to the depths of the sea and his home in a living submarine. Dark walls of a whale's insides couldn't block the light of God's wisdom from Jonah's searching mind. What had made sense three days ago looked today like worthless idolatry. Jonah had slammed the gates of grace on sinful Nineveh. He had determined they weren't worth saving. Three days later this waterlogged wanderer concluded that the Lord was indeed God. Jonah made promises and sang songs of praise to his God. Then God told the fish to cough up this repentant roomer. Jonah hit land with a running start and a softened heart.

Question: Most of us love to sing in the shower, but how well do we sing in hot or deep water?

Faithlift: Your song from deep waters draws seekers to God.

NOVEMBER 20

Then the word of the LORD *came to Jonah, a second time. Jonah obeyed the word of the* LORD *and went to Nineveh. Jonah 3:1, 3*

Further reading: Jonah 3

Thank God for a second chance! This time a wiser, though waterlogged, Jonah jumped at God's offer and took off for Nineveh. He preached, and the people repented. "The Ninevites believed God. They declared a fast, and all of them, from the greatest to the least, put on sackcloth" (v. 5). God's great love for sulky Jonah and a sinful city resulted in second chances for both.

Question: Where would you be without a second chance from God?

Faithlift: You give joy to God when you offer a second chance to a brother or sister.

NOVEMBER 21

When God saw what they did and how they turned from their evil ways, he had compassion and did not bring upon them the destruction he had threatened. But Jonah was greatly displeased and became angry. He prayed to the LORD, *"O* LORD, *is this not what I said when I was still at home? That is why I was so quick to flee to Tarshish. I knew that you are a gracious and com-*

passionate God, slow to anger and abounding in love, a God who relents from sending calamity." Jonah 3:10–4:2

Further reading: Jonah 3–4

The wealth and wickedness of the Ninevites stirred Jonah's bigotry. Jonah, like too many of us, sought to hoard the good news of grace for himself and his people. Nineveh's nickname was the Robber City, because it "robbed and overran other countries to enrich itself" (p. 1681, The Thompson Chain Reference Bible NIV). Jonah didn't want them stealing his God, too. It was their turn to pay. But God's ways, thankfully, are not ours or Jonah's. And the Ninevites, as undeserving as we are, found the gates of grace open to a people on their knees.

Question: Where would we be if God gave us what we deserved?

Faithlift: Share your faith with a neighboring "Ninevite" today.

NOVEMBER 22

But the LORD said, "You have been concerned about this vine, though you did not tend it or make it grow. It sprang up overnight and died overnight. But Nineveh has more than a hundred and twenty thousand people who cannot tell their right hand from their left, and many cattle as well. Should I not be concerned about that great city?" Jonah 4:10–11

Further reading: Jonah 4

Do you allow your children to disagree with you at home? Take a minute to examine this scene between Jonah and God, his Father. Jonah obeyed the second time around. Do your kids get a second chance? Jonah complained and expressed suicidal thoughts when God showed compassion on sinful Nineveh. But God didn't beat him with words or whip him. He asked his sulky son a question. "Have you any right to be angry?" (v. 4). Jonah didn't bother to answer. He shuffled off to a place outside the city, "made himself a shelter, sat in its shade and waited to see what would happen to the city" (v. 5). How did God respond to His pathetic prophet? "The LORD God provided a vine and made it grow up over Jonah to give shade for his head to ease his discomfort, and Jonah was very happy about the vine" (v. 6). How do you handle the discomfort of a member of your family? The next day God sent a worm to chew up the vine, which left Jonah in the scorching sun, wanting to die again (see vv. 7–8). God asked Jonah another question—a variation on the first one. "Do you have a right to be angry about the vine?" (v. 9). Jonah never answered either question, as far as we know. God must have felt it was more important for us to know His questions than to know the answers.

Question: How safe is your home for people with a different set of questions and answers?

Faithlift: Healthy families encourage their children to ask good questions instead of training them to give good answers.

NOVEMBER 23

He [the Lord] will judge between many peoples and will settle disputes for strong nations far and wide. They will beat their swords into plowshares and their spears into pruning hooks. Nation will not take up sword against nation, nor will they train for war anymore. Micah 4:3

Further reading: Micah 2–4

The evening news highlights the threat of war in the Middle East. Newspapers and magazines show fearful faces, young and old. While war machines and money pour into the Middle East, one wonders about an Armageddon (see Revelation 16)—one last battle before God calls "Enough!" Though we don't know when God will return, we do know He will. Until God calls and comes for His children, remember the picture of peace in Micah 4:3 and reach out to your neighbors with God's good news.

Question: Who comes to mind when you think of reaching out with God's good news?

Faithlift: We don't know when God will return, but we do know He will return.

NOVEMBER 24

He has showed you, O man, what is good. And what does the LORD require of you? To act justly and to love mercy and to walk humbly with your God.
Micah 6:8

Further reading: Micah 6

These are simple requirements to understand: act justly, love mercy, walk humbly with your God. But sometimes simple is not easy.

Question: What's on your "to do" list that requires justice, mercy, or humility?

Faithlift: God never requires anything of you that goes beyond His resources for you.

NOVEMBER 25

A man's enemies are the members of his own household.
Micah 7:6

Further reading: Micah 7

Have you ever felt this way? God, your Father, understands the pain of rebellious children, of unfaithful lovers, or of difficult family members. What do you do? Micah continues, "But as for me, I watch in hope for the LORD, I wait for God my Savior; my God will hear me" (v. 7). So you watch and wait. But who you watch while you wait determines your success in handling the situation from start to finish. Shift your focus from your enemies to your eternal Father, who understands best the high cost of unconditional love.

Question: How do you respond to in-house opposition?

Faithlift: You're not alone in your home; God is with you.

NOVEMBER 26

Do not gloat over me, my enemy! Though I have fallen, I will rise. Though I sit in darkness, the LORD *will be my light. Micah 7:8*

Further reading: Micah 7

What encouragement to all of us with skinned knees, bruised hearts, and dark memories! As morning follows night, so rising follows falling for God's children. The enemy of God and His children lurks outside unemployment offices, in dank prison cells, in hospital corridors, and in crowded courtrooms, snickering at their distress. But sneers slide from his evil countenance when God's broken, downtrodden children cry to Him from gutters, prison bars, or hospital cribsides. These are not the prayers and praises of the triumphant but the sobs of the penitent, the plodding seekers, and faithful followers of God. And the enemy knows better than to gloat. Even he knows up from down.

Question: What do you do when you've fallen?

Faithlift: Though you have fallen, you will rise.

NOVEMBER 27

You will again have compassion on us; you will tread our sins underfoot and hurl all our iniquities into the depths of the sea. Micah 7:19

Further reading: Micah 7

Someone once said, "God may hurl our sins into the sea, but the problem is that the enemy has deep sea divers." The enemy can fill net after net with our sins and haul them to the foot of God's throne, but no harm will come to God's children. While Satan, our enemy, is busy tattling, God is treading our sins underfoot. The enemy's words can never harm God's children unless we believe his words more than God's. We choose daily which words we will live by: accusations of a defeated enemy or the affirmations of a compassionate, merciful, and forgiving God. What God says, He will do. Unfortunately, the enemy knows that better than we.

Question: Whose words are you living by today?

Faithlift: The treasure of God's forgiveness can never be stolen from God's children by an enemy diver.

NOVEMBER 28

The LORD is good, a refuge in times of trouble. He cares for those who trust in him, but with an overwhelming flood he will make an end of Nineveh; he will pursue his foes into darkness. Nahum 1:7

Further reading: Nahum 1–3

In the middle of a chapter describing God's anger against His enemies and His power over nature sits a tiny verse about God's protection for His trusting children. Like a small oasis in a vast desert or a thread of light in thick darkness comes God's commitment to care for His children. To His enemies God sends "an overwhelming flood." To His children He remains "a refuge in times of trouble." God, who is good, cannot treat His children and His enemies the same.

Question: Why would anyone want to be God's enemy?

Faithlift: Trusting God doesn't save you from trouble but it provides "a refuge in times of trouble."

NOVEMBER 29

How long, O LORD, must I call for help, but you do not listen? Or cry out to you, "Violence!" but you do not save? Why do you make me look at injustice? Why do you tolerate wrong? Destruction and violence are before me; there is strife, and conflict abounds. Therefore the law is paralyzed, and justice never prevails. The wicked hem in the righteous, so that justice is perverted. Habakkuk 1:2–4

Further reading: Habakkuk 1–3

This description of rampant violence sounds like New York, Los Angeles, or Chicago. These questions also plague God's children in Cambodia, Russia, South Africa, Chile, and the rest of the world. The sounds of conflict and perverted justice prevail in the Middle East and on Midtown subways in New York City. A violent virus infects the people of this earth, and thinking people question the whereabouts of God. No simple answers passed from God's mouth to Habakkuk's ears, nor to ours. For our part, we can only respond as did Habakkuk, "I will stand at my watch" (2:1). With or without answers, we are to stand and wait, hating evil, loving people, trusting God to be God. And one day, when we least expect it, God will strike down the capitals and villages of the earth, and "the earth will be filled with the knowledge of the glory of the LORD, as the waters cover the sea" (2:14). Until then, God prefers honest questions to apathy.

Question: What questions do you have?

Faithlift: God's silence does not mean He does not listen or care.

NOVEMBER 30

LORD, I have heard of your fame; I stand in awe of your deeds, O LORD. Renew them in our day, in our time make them known; in wrath remember mercy.
Habakkuk 3:2

Further reading: Habakkuk 1–3

The prophet Habakkuk, heavily burdened by the violence and injustice around him (see Habakkuk 1), still reflected on the awesomeness of God. He didn't just stand his watch; he stood in awe of God's deeds. Reflecting on God made Habakkuk long for revival. "Do it again, God," he prayed. God's still recruiting and training men and women, like Habakkuk, who will continue to stand and cry, "Do it again, God."

Question: What do you find awesome about God?

Faithlift: Praise the God who remembers to be merciful, the God who revives His people.

December

December 1

Though the fig tree does not bud and there are no grapes on the vines, though the olive crop fails and the fields produce no food, though there are no sheep in the pen and no cattle in the stalls, yet I will rejoice in the LORD, I will be joyful in God my Savior.
Habakkuk 3:17–18

Further reading: Habakkuk 3

Habakkuk took a realistic look at life without the goodies: no figs, grapes, olives, sheep, or cattle. No food and no job. Yet! Habakkuk hung on by a *yet*. Habakkuk had no control over famine and unproductive fields, over dead, stolen, or lost sheep and cattle. But he could choose his response to these disasters. Habakkuk willed to rejoice and to be joyful in God, no matter what. Habakkuks seem rare in our culture. We need more men and women with confident trust in God, with or without His material blessings.

Question: Why do you trust God?

Faithlift: Faithful followers give God their trust, just for nothing.

December 2

The Sovereign LORD is my strength; he makes my feet like the feet of a deer, he enables me to go on the heights.
Habakkuk 3:19

Further reading: Habakkuk 3

Moving up requires the Lord, not a ladder.

Question: Have you set your sights high enough?

Faithlift: Don't settle for the lowlands when God has made you for the heights.

December 3

At that time I will search Jerusalem with lamps and punish those who are complacent, who are like wine left on its dregs, who think, "The LORD will do nothing, either good or bad." Zephaniah 1:12

Further reading: Zephaniah 1–3

Complacency characterizes our culture and sometimes our churches. Many give no thought one way or another to God. Yet, sprinkled among the complacent are God's committed followers. They praise God and trust Him, seasoning the earth. God's remnant halts total decay with a touch of salt. It's difficult to remain bland when surrounded by salty disciples of the living God.

Question: Why are the numbers of committed followers shrinking?

Faithlift: God's committed followers are the salt of the earth.

December 4

The LORD your God is with you, he is mighty to save. He will take great delight in you, he will quiet you with his love, he will rejoice over you with singing. Zephaniah 3:17

Further reading: Zephaniah 3

Children of all ages love a song, especially one sung by a loving parent. Imagine your Father God singing! The God who is "mighty to save" is also delighted to "sing." The Lord of the lullaby "will rejoice over you with singing." Minimize the world's distraction so you won't miss His music.

Question: How does music affect you?

Faithlift: Listen for the songs of your Savior today.

December 5

"I will rescue the lame and gather those who have been scattered. I will give them praise and

honor in every land where they were put to shame. At that time I will gather you; at that time I will bring you home. I will give you honor and praise among all the peoples of the earth when I restore your fortunes before your very eyes," says the LORD. *Zephaniah 3:19–20*

Further reading: Zephaniah 3

Israel—lame, insulted, attacked, and conquered—heard the words all lost children long to hear: their Father was coming to gather them up and bring them home. No more shame or rebuke from their enemies. God, their Father, also promised "honor and praise among all the peoples of the earth" *when* He restored their fortunes (v. 20). God did not say *if*, He said *when*. This promised fortune was not trinkets, strands of pearls, or prized gems, but people. All hostages were heading home.

Question: Are there words you long to hear from your Father?

Faithlift: God's promises to His obedient children are a matter of *when*, not *if*.

DECEMBER 6

Then the word of the LORD *came through the prophet Haggai: "Is it a time for you yourselves to be living in your paneled houses, while this house remains a ruin?" Haggai 1:3–4*

Further reading: Haggai 1

The temple in Jerusalem lay in ruins. Some of God's chidren stumbled on her stones as they meandered to the market. The market provided beautiful adornments for their houses, while God's house remained in shambles. But God grabbed their attention with a question. "Is it a time for you yourselves to be living in your paneled houses, while this house remains a ruin?" God's neglected house stood in stark contrast to their well-tended homes. The people heard God's probing question because Haggai, God's prophet, heard God's question and dared to pass it on to a preoccupied people. The restoration and rebuilding work began in God's children and spread to His temple.

Question: How much attention do you give to matters outside your home and job?

Faithlift: The more we listen, the more clearly we'll understand God's heart and tend God's timeless treasures.

December 7

Now this is what the LORD Almighty says: "Give careful thought to your ways. You have planted much, but have harvested little. You eat, but never have enough. You drink, but never have your fill. You put on clothes, but are not warm. You earn wages, only to put them in a purse with holes in it." Haggai 1:5–6

Further reading: Haggai 1

Many of us find that we do not have enough money to carry us through the month. Conspicuous consumption plagues our culture and even drives some people to commit crimes against those they supposedly love. It's time we gave careful thought to our ways. Is it possible that our overworked, unfulfilled status finds its roots in the fact that we neglect God's concerns? A materialistic culture thrives on buying, but God's economy thrives on bowing. When God's children bend their ears to hear and bow their knees to pray, God sets in motion returns for our investment that are unmatched by the world's warranties.

Question: Is it time to "give careful thought to your ways"?

Faithlift: Investments in God's concerns pay eternal dividends.

December 8

"You expected much, but see, it turned out to be little. What you brought home, I blew away. Why?" declares the LORD Almighty. "Because of my house, which remains a ruin, while each

of you is busy with his own house." Haggai 1:9

Further reading: Haggai 1

There will never be enough for those who are preoccupied with accumulating the world's goods. God has used natural events like droughts to stir His children toward reform. Today, God may even use the Internal Revenue Service to get our attention and turn our focus from filling our pockets to fulfilling His purposes.

Question: How does God get your attention?

Faithlift: Financial planning and wise investments begin with God.

DECEMBER 9

"Be strong, all you people of the land," declares the LORD, "and work. For I am with you," declares the LORD Almighty. Haggai 2:4

Further reading: Haggai 2

God never recruits without the required resources, nor will He waste His strength on the shiftless. Rather, as we work, we find His power and His presence. God's concern for building His children preceded His plans to rebuild His temple. As God's children obediently worked to rebuild His temple, they found God restoring them as well.

Question: What are you facing that requires God's power and presence?

Faithlift: As you do God's work today, God is also at work in you.

DECEMBER 10

The LORD was very angry with your forefathers. Therefore tell the people: This is what the LORD Almighty says: "Return to me," declares the LORD Almighty, "and I will return to you." Zechariah 1:2–3

Further reading: Zechariah 1

Few of us come from good families, and even those who do can only trace that good heritage back so far. A careful look inward finds us falling short of God's mark, blighting the best of family trees. To all who long to begin a more healthy branch God says, "Return to me and I will return to you." And if we return now, younger and yet unborn generations will live to thank us.

Question: Can you think of a better inheritance to pass on to the next generation?

Faithlift: There is no better season to begin a branch of righteousness than right now.

DECEMBER 11

"And I myself will be a wall of fire around it," declares the LORD, "and I will be its glory within." Zechariah 2:5

Further reading: Zechariah 2

Walls provided security for a city and its people, but God had sent word to His children that "Jerusalem will be a city without walls because of the great number of men and livestock in it" (v. 4). God's children would have been terrified to live in such an indefensible city, so God drew up a defense stronger than stone. God promised to wall them in with the fire of His presence outside and the Shekinah glory within. To get to them, you had to go through God. That's an uncrackable security system.

Question: Would you like to tap into this system?

Faithlift: God's presence is your protection.

DECEMBER 12

For this is what the LORD Almighty says: . . . "Whoever touches you touches the apple of his eye." Zechariah 2:8

Further reading: Zechariah 2

Parents, especially new ones, whip out wallets packed with photos to show off the apple(s) of their eyes. How proud they are of their two-legged treasures! Little folks grow best in safe, nurturing environments where they know they belong, are loved, and occupy the prestigious position as the apple of somebody's eye. When God refers to His children as the apple of His eye, He likens us to the pupil of the eye. We instinctively protect our eyes from harm. God sees His children as vulnerable and as sensitive as the pupil of an eye. We never outgrow our need to belong, to feel loved, and to know we are special to someone. God, our Father, maker, and sustainer, knows this and more about us. How awesome to think that God has chosen us and protects us like the apple of His eye.

Question: Can you picture your face in God's wallet?

Faithlift: My, how your Father loves you!

DECEMBER 13

Now Joshua was dressed in filthy clothes as he stood before the angel. The angel said to those who were standing before him, "Take off his filthy clothes." Zechariah 3:3

Further reading: Zechariah 3

One look in the mirrors and closets of our lives and we shudder with the realization that our clothes are filthy. Like Joshua the high priest, we stand covered in sin and shame. Joshua's enemy and ours stands at our elbows, tattling to God. Satan, the accuser, never quits trying to get God to change His mind about us. But God also never fails to exchange the rags of the penitent for robes of righteousness. Praise God, who offers forgiveness to the filthy and who wraps us in His grace.

Question: Who designs your wardrobe?

Faithlift: You can spot God's children by their garments of grace and robes of righteousness.

December 14

So he said to me, "This is the word of the LORD to Zerubbabel: 'Not by might nor by power, by by my Spirit,' says the LORD Almighty." Zechariah 4:6

Further reading: Zechariah 4

Prophets like Zechariah, priests like Zerubbabel, and people like Nehemiah worked hard to rebuild the temple in Jerusalem. At times opposition must have loomed larger than the construction project. What was true for God's chidren then is true for us today. In the middle of the mountainous climb to completion, we need to hear God's words, "Not by might nor by power, but by my Spirit." We must do what we can and trust the rest to God.

Question: How does God fit into your drive to the finish?

Faithlift: Remember today to trust God's Spirit for strength to complete your tasks.

December 15

Who despises the day of small things? Zechariah 4:10

Further reading: Zechariah 4

Raising Jerusalem from the rubble required both small and large contributions. Snickering scoffers probably ridiculed the wobbly-legged old and clumsy young workers who did their part to rebuild the temple. It is natural to look for large, highly visible ways to participate. God needed to remind His priest Zerubbabel that nothing and no one was too small for God to use. Today, there are still those who snicker, spit, and scoff as God's children give what they can to the work of His kingdom. The same enemy slithers up to discourage and disperse God's workers. But God's construction continues, carried on best at times by little people in small ways.

Question: What are some small things you are doing or

can do to build up one of God's children or to encourage His church?

Faithlift: Look for little ways to serve your great God.

December 16

Then the word of the LORD *Almighty came to me: "Ask all the people of the land and the priests, 'When you fasted and mourned in the fifth and seventh months for the past seventy years, was it really for me that you fasted?'" Zechariah 7:4–5*

Further reading: Zechariah 7

Seventy years totaled a major chunk of life in which significant days had been devoted to dutiful fasting and mourning—and then God questioned their motives! Sometimes it is difficult to distinguish between what we do for God and what we do for ourselves. Throughout the Old Testament God pressed His children to catch His heart more than read His lips. While there was no discrepancy between God's words and actions, His children sometimes stressed the letter of the law and missed its application. When it's easier to do without food than to dole that food out to the needy, some questions need addressing. "Was it really for me that you fasted?"

Question: What questions do you need to ask?

Faithlift: God will speak to our hearts when it's time to fast or time to feed others.

December 17

This is what the LORD *Almighty says: "Administer true justice; show mercy and compassion to one another." Zechariah 7:9*

Further reading: Zechariah 7

Some of us find it easier to fast for God than to focus on others through administering justice and showing mercy or compassion. That fast God's children questioned had begun seventy years earlier to mourn their captivity, the sins of their fathers, and the temple's destruction by the

Babylonians. Now, since the temple was almost rebuilt, many questioned why they should continue the practice. The people didn't want to decide for themselves, so they inquired of the ruling authorities in Jerusalem. The prophet Zechariah sent back a strong response from God, questioning the motives behind their fasting. God cared more for compassion than ceremony, more for mercy than for going through the motions. God's balky children needed to learn that loving obedience to God's Word, not abstinence, pleased God's heart. We must learn the same lesson.

Question: Are you trying to win God's favor through doing *without* instead of doing *what* He has commanded?

Faithlift: Loving obedience to God's words puts the right motive behind the motions of this day.

DECEMBER 18

But they refused to pay attention; stubbornly they turned their backs and stopped up their ears. They made their hearts as hard as flint and would not listen to the law or to the words that the LORD *Almighty had sent by his Spirit through the earlier prophets. So the* LORD *Almighty was very angry. Zechariah 7:11–12*

Further reading: Zechariah 7

Through Zechariah God described His children as a stubborn ox, balky, refusing to allow the yoke on its shoulders. He pictured His children with hard, unteachable hearts and clogged ears. They preferred to do *without* rather than to do *what* God required: administer justice and show mercy and compassion to others.

Question: How different are you from those Israelites?

Faithlift: The tender heart obeys God's tough commands.

DECEMBER 19

"When I called, they did not listen; so when they called, I would

not listen," says the LORD Almighty. Zechariah 7:13

Further reading: Zechariah 7

What if God treated us as we treat Him?

Question: How well do you listen to God?

Faithlift: Listen for God's words to you today.

DECEMBER 20

This is how they made the pleasant land desolate. Zechariah 7:14

Further reading: Zechariah 7

Choice by choice the Israelites turned their Promised Land into a desolate place. Disobedience to God's laws left them vulnerable to conquering armies, who replaced their celebrations with captivity. The people God had gathered in love He now scattered in wrath. They, and generations that followed, paid a high price for having their way.

Question: Are you making any pleasant places desolate through selfish choices?

Faithlift: Obey God and feel His pleasure and presence in your place today.

DECEMBER 21

This is what the LORD Almighty says: "Once again men and women of ripe old age will sit in the streets of Jerusalem, each with cane in hand because of his age. The city streets will be filled with boys and girls playing there." Zechariah 8:4–5

Further reading: Zechariah 8

Through Zechariah God described city life for His children when He returns to dwell in Zion. The two most neglected groups in society, elderly people and young children, will thrive in God's city. Powerful business and industry lobbies will take a back seat to society's powerless old folks and children. Imagine New York with cars, taxis, and buses curbed so children could play safely in the streets. Imagine our government using its brains and billions of dollars to tend to those who serve no practical function in society. Imagine God's judgment on a society that routinely aborts the young and shelves the elderly. The higher our view of God, the higher our view of life at both ends of the spectrum.

Question: How does God's city compare with yours?

Faithlift: Look for ways to serve those our society tends to shelve.

DECEMBER 22

Let us go with you, because we have heard that God is with you. Zechariah 8:23

Further reading: Zechariah 8

A heart that is hungry to know God resides in each person. When others see God, Immanuel, in us, they want to come along. What they hear and see as they accompany us determines if they want to join us for the rest of the journey home.

Question: Is someone following you?

Faithlift: Your life can cause someone to come along today as you celebrate this advent season, the coming of Immanuel.

DECEMBER 23

"A son honors his father, and a servant his master. If I am a father, where is the honor due me? If I am a master, where is the respect due me?" says the LORD Almighty. Malachi 1:6

Further reading: Malachi 1

In this season of both love and greed, we would do well to examine these questions from God to His priests and the whole nation of Israel. If our fathers on earth deserve respect, how much more honor belongs to our heavenly Father! We show honor with our ways more than our words. What we do demonstrates what we believe. Check your uses of time and money during this holy season and see who you are honoring.

Question: What gift are you giving your Father this Christmas?

Faithlift: You are the best gift to God.

DECEMBER 24

"When you bring blind animals for sacrifice, is that not wrong? When you sacrifice crippled or diseased animals, is that not wrong? Try offering them to your governor! Would he be pleased with you? Would he accept you?" says the LORD Almighty. Malachi 1:8

Further reading: Malachi 1

God wants our delight in Him, not duty to Him, to motivate us to give our best. The priests and people of Israel mocked God with their sick sacrifices and low standards. They did what the law required, but their hearts were hard. Too many of God's North American children will feel exhausted and frustrated at the end of this day. Material gods will have drained their bodies and bank accounts. On Christmas Eve we are apt to be wrapping the best for ourselves and giving the leftovers to God. And our Father God will stand silent, sidelined beside our festive tables and gorgeous Christmas trees, piled high with packages. He will watch us scramble for the best while He strokes a worn teddy bear with one arm and no eyes.

Question: How do you maintain God's standards in our materialistic culture?

Faithlift: God's gifts never need exchanging.

DECEMBER 25

"Cursed is the cheat who has an acceptable male in his flock and vows to give it, but then sacrifices a blemished animal to the Lord. For I am a great king," says the LORD Almighty, "and

my name is to be feared among the nations." Malachi 1:14

Further reading: Malachi 10

God hates cheats, especially religious cheats, who work so hard at looking good. Christmas reminds some of us to be religious. We ceremoniously go to church, deck our mantles with manger scenes, and listen to carols sung by our favorite entertainers. But all too soon the tree becomes firewood and turkey dregs fill the dog's dish. Toys break, and yesterday's promises pile up with the trash until Easter, when we rev up our religious engines and try again. Deep inside, our hungry hearts crave a living relationship with God, not one more attempt at being a religious cheat. We're tired of taking back the acceptable and passing off the blemished as good enough to get God off our backs. When times get tough, we promise God our best; but we take it back in better times. A half-hearted gift is not a gift; it's only one more variation on religious cheating. You are the only acceptable gift to God this Christmas Day. He wants you to give Him your hungry heart.

Question: What do you have to lose if you give God your whole heart?

Faithlift: God waits to give you the gift of real life—and more true treasures than you could ask for or imagine.

DECEMBER 26

You have wearied the LORD with your words. Malachi 2:17

Further reading: Malachi 2

Most of us grow weary of words from time to time. Words bombard us from television, radio, tapes, newspapers, magazines, telephones, and people within sight or shouting range. Throughout the Christmas season we hear words sung. Our ears bristle as children whine and adults manipulate their words to gain advantage. Some words form prayers. The prayers of the truly repentant never tire God's ears, but complaining, unthankful words weary the Lord and others. Honest cries and whispered confessions remain welcome sounds to God; those who seek to impress God with their words find Him tired of their talk.

Question: How would you rate your words? Wearisome? Welcome?

Faithlift: You are capable of refreshing God and others with your words.

December 27

I the LORD do not change.
Malachi 3:6

Further reading: Malachi 3

Change marks our bodies, relationships, and responsibilities. Some of God's chidren have experienced devastating changes this past year. Disease, divorce, and death are only a few. Perched precariously between the year almost past and a new year, we long for something or someone unchanging. The good news is that God does not change. The bad news is that God's standards for holy living do not change, either. Through Malachi God warned His children of judgment for their unfaithfulness. We and our children need to be reminded that the fuzzy guidelines of this world are not God's alternative lifestyles. His commandments remain commandments. But those who return to Him, who trust and obey, will find Him a faithful Father in a world of flux.

Question: How do you respond to change?

Faithlift: No matter what changes in or around you, God remains the same.

December 28

"Will a man rob God? Yet you rob me. But you ask, 'How do we rob you?' In tithes and offerings. You are under a curse—the whole nation of you—because you are robbing me. Bring the whole tithe into the storehouse, that there may be food in my house. Test me in this," says the LORD Almighty, "and see if I

will not throw open the floodgates of heaven and pour out so much blessing that you will not have room enough for it." Malachi 3:8–10

Further reading: Malachi 3

Many of us use the days between Christmas and New Years to reflect, set goals, and make resolutions. While we contemplate waste and waist cutting measures, we would do well to consider the ways we handle God's gifts to us. Did we rob God? Perhaps we dammed the "floodgates of heaven" with fearful hoarding or blatant materialism and cheated ourselves of the joys of glad giving. Perhaps we robbed God of the delight of flooding us with blessings. It's worth more than a passing thought on a day in December.

Question: What does it mean to rob God?

Faithlift: Wholehearted giving to God releases wholehearted blessing from God.

December 29

Then those who feared the LORD talked with each other, and the LORD listened and heard. A scroll of remembrance was written in his presence concerning those who feared the LORD and honored his name. Malachi 3:16

Further reading: Malachi 3

God's rebukes hung on Israel's ears like a gavel-pounded verdict. Accusations of robbing God, of fasting and mourning for nothing, did little for the Israelites' sense of religious esteem. Some questioned any gain in carrying out God's requirements. Others feared God and talked with each other. Who we talk *to* and what we talk *about* can determine vastly different outcomes, some with eternal consequences. God never destroys people for asking questions of Him, neither does He defend those who avoid His questions and ignore His answers.

Question: Can you honor God's name, even when you feel like the wicked prosper and "What did we gain carrying out [God's] requirements"? (v. 14).

Faithlift: Honor God today with your honest questions and obedience to what you know.

December 30

"They [those who fear the LORD and honor his name] will be mine," says the LORD Almighty, "in the day when I make up my treasured possession. I will spare them, just as in compassion a man spares his son who serves him. And you will again see the distinction between the righteous and the wicked, between those who serve God and those who do not." Malachi 3:17–18

Further reading: Malachi 3

Only the truly righteous or self-righteous welcome a day of distinctions. Too many of us are too godly to be comfortable in our standard-lacking society and too ungodly to be eager for a day of distinctions. On this day before year's end we would do well to kneel and repent of our contributions to clouded standards within the church and culture. We need to model what we demand of others and move into the new year committed to following God's standards for holy living.

Question: How could you clear up some clouded distinctions in your area of influence?

Faithlift: You can do much to rid our environment of spiritual smog.

December 31

See, I will send you the prophet Elijah before that great and dreadful day of the LORD comes. He will turn the hearts of the fathers to their children, and the hearts of the children to their fathers. Malachi 4:6

Further reading: Malachi 4 and Luke 1:5–17

Newspapers, television, and movies portray nightmarish accounts of abuse by parents of children and by children of parents. The home as a safe place in a scary world seems endangered, like a great white rhino. Powerful forces, both visible and invisible, nibble and gnaw at the family and twist the heart to do dark deeds. It seems unnatural for parents and children to love each other and normal for sick relationships to thrive in many families. We need supernatural help to love each other. Real love does not come naturally. We need a Savior, a Messiah, to turn our hearts to our Father God. We need a new heart and the power of His Spirit to turn our hearts toward our children and our parents. That Savior has come. His name is Jesus. No family or individual need live in the dark or spend one more futile day stuffing synthetic food into a hungry heart. This New Year can be different. It's your choice.

Question: What are you hoping will be different about this New Year?

Faithlift: Trust the God who will make the difference in this year by making a difference in you.

About the Author

Jan Jensen Carlberg heard the stories of God's love and justice as a little girl growing up in a pastor's home. Her parents, Harold and Margaret Jensen, loved God and their three children. As Jan grew into adulthood, she never lost her hungry heart for God and His word. Her love for teaching has lead to service in a number of ways: teaching English and speech/drama in junior high and high school, Sunday school, and in small and large community Bible studies for women. Jan also served as the director of orientation for new students, campus activities coordinator and later as the assistant chaplain at Gordon College. Until choosing to focus on speaking and writing, Jan was the director of women's ministries at Grace Chapel in Lexington, MA.

Jan met her husband, Dr. R. Judson Carlberg, at Wheaton College in Illinois. For fourteen years he was the academic dean at Gordon College in Wenham, MA. Early in 1990, he assumed the duties of the senior vice president for development at Gordon. They have two children: Heather is a sophomore at Brown University in Rhode Island and Chad is a freshman at Gordon College.

The typeface for the text of this book is *Palatino*. This type—best known as a contemporary *italic* typeface—was a post-World War II design crafted by the talented young German calligrapher Hermann Zapf. For inspiration, Zapf drew upon the writing legacy of a group of Italian Renaissance writing masters, in which the typeface's namesake, Giovanni Battista Palatino, was numbered. Giovanni Palatino's *Libro nuovo d'imparare a scrivera* was published in Rome in 1540 and became one of the most used, wide-ranging writing manuals of the sixteenth century. Zapf was an apt student of the European masters, and contemporary *Palatino* is one of his contributions to modern typography.

Substantive Editing:
Michael S. Hyatt

Copy Editing:
Peggy Moon

Dust Jacket Design:
Steve Diggs & Friends
Nashville, Tennessee

Page Composition:
Xerox Ventura Publisher
Printware 720 IQ Laser Printer

Printing and Binding:
Maple-Vail Printing Group
York, Pennsylvania

Dust Jacket Printing:
Strine Printing Company
York, Pennsylvania